EAGLE FIVE-LINEBACKER DEFENSE

Fritz Shurmur

Harding Press
Haworth, New Jersey 07641

To Peggy Jane, whose patience, understanding, and support through all the good and especially the not-so-good times make her an incredibly special coach's wife and mother. To our kids—Sally Ann the writer, Scott the doctor, and Susie the teacher—who have been and always will be great sources of pride to us.

To my mother and father, Len and Katie Shurmur, who worked and sacrificed all their lives to give me opportunities they never had. I will always be grateful.

To the many coaches and players I have been privileged to work with over the years. They are the reason going to work every day has been so enjoyable.

Library of Congress Cataloging-in-Publication Data

Shurmur, Fritz.
    The Eagle five-linebacker defense / Fritz Shurmur.
      p. cm.
    ISBN 0–9624779–4–X
    1. Football—Defense.   2. Philadelphia Eagles (Football team)
  I. Title.
  GV951.18.S49   1993
  796.332'2—dc20   92–38945
                                         CIP

ISBN 0-9624779-4-X

Printed in the United States of America

HARDING PRESS
P. O. Box 141
Haworth, NJ 07641

Books by and for the coaching profession

Contents

About the Author

A veteran of 18 seasons in the NFL, nearly 40 years in coaching, Fritz Shurmur is a staunch believer in the potential for greatness possible when people work hard together. His coaching philosophy is rooted in commitment to a team, its objectives and collective goals.

The Eagle Five-Linebacker Defense is about the necessary factors in keeping the opponent out of the end zone—achieving Shurmur's "11 men to the football" approach. It is written for the football coach at any level of play, regardless of coaching experience or philosophy. Although this book is about a specific, unique, and innovative scheme, its defensive principles, techniques, and drills are applicable to any defensive scheme, regardless of level.

Shurmur is recognized as a leading teacher of zone pass coverages; he has also been most prominent in development of the hands technique for defensive linemen. The method of phase teaching he developed in the early 1960s is a proven way to teach defensive linemen to play on the line of scrimmage.

He has pioneered the use of unique combinations of personnel. While with the LA Rams, he was one of the first to utilize the nickel 33 scheme in first- and second-down situations. He has pioneered the development of unique multi-linebacker schemes in various down-and-distance situations.

A Michigan native, Shurmur is a graduate of Albion College, with an undergraduate degree in physical education and a master's degree in educational administration. He earned four varsity letters in both football and baseball and was named all-conference as a second baseman in 1954. He captained the 1953 football squad, earning all-league honors at center, and was named team and league most valuable player.

Shurmur's coaching career began with a grad assistantship at Albion, serving as assistant football coach and swimming coach through 1961, when he became defensive line coach at the University of Wyoming. Under his tutelage, the Pokes became the only major college football team to win as many as two defensive titles during the 1960s—rushing and total defense. In 1966 and 1967, the Cowboys led the nation in rushing defense and in 1968 ranked first in total defense.

After serving as head coach at Wyoming from 1971–1974, Shurmur entered the NFL as defensive line coach with the Detroit Lions. He served as defensive coordinator in 1977.

Four years in New England followed, as defensive line coach, then as defensive coordinator. In 1978, with an 11–5 record, the Patriots won the AFC East division title, while Shurmur's Patriot defense led the NFL the next year with 57 quarterback sacks.

In 1982, Shurmur was named defensive line coach by the LA Rams. When John Robinson became head coach in 1983, Shurmur was promoted to defensive coordinator. The Rams led the NFL in quarterback sacks in 1985, finishing fifth in total defense both that season and the next.

Shurmur again improvised in 1989 when, due to injuries, he was forced to use linebackers as down linemen. Using only linebackers and defensive backs, his unit allowed only three running backs to gain 100 yards, finished fifth in the NFC with 42 sacks, and led the Rams to a pair of postseason victories.

In 1991, Shurmur joined the Phoenix Cardinals. Despite using seven new starters his defenders allowed 52 fewer points than the previous season and overall shared the league-low by allowing just 12 touchdown passes. The Cardinal defense produced 37 opponent fumbles; its 21 fumble recoveries ranked second in the conference and third in the league.

1

Introduction: The Eagle Defense

The Eagle defense represents a unique concept of defensive football. Radically moving away from the traditional use of three or four defensive linemen, this scheme utilizes only two, and although it is possible to play the Eagle with three defensive linemen, the versatility and possible variations are unlimited when the combination of two defensive linemen and five linebackers is used. Although the alignment is not original, certainly the utilization of personnel is.

The defense is named for an alignment used by the defensive tackle. Since I started coaching over 38 years ago I have always referred to the alignment of the defensive tackle when he is lined up on the outside. shoulder of the offensive guard as an Eagle alignment or position. I am told this alignment was originally used by Greasy Neale when he coached the Philadelphia Eagles. He used this alignment in a defense we called the 53, or the 53 defense. I think every defensive notebook I ever had anything to do with has had this Eagle alignment of the tackles as part of the variations we taught. So, it was relatively simple to come up with a name for our unique scheme that utilized an alignment we already had a term for in our defensive book.

I believe this defense offers options not available in other schemes. The utilization of two outside linebackers as pass rushers and run reactors on every down is unique. It is unique in two ways. One, the fact that they line up with so much width is different than most schemes. Also, the fact that by assignment and alignment they are able to rush so hard on every down represents a radical departure from traditional schemes.

The two tackles in the defense are penetrators, pass rushers, and run reactors on every down. Although this alignment and responsibility occur in some schemes, there is none where these players have the opportunity to exercise this type of play with such regularity.

Another of the unique positions in the Eagle is that of nose linebacker. This player is used as a defensive lineman, run defender and pass rusher, and as a linebacker pass defender. The ability to move him on and off the line of scrimmage as well as the changing of his responsibilities from pass rusher to pass dropper are huge factors in reducing predictability. The value of this type of defensive edge cannot be minimized.

The strong safety position is different in this defense for many reasons. One is that he lines up on the weak side of the formation most of the time. Another is that he lines up within five yards of the line of scrimmage most of the time. This means he must be able to play like a linebacker in many situations. Included in these areas are run fills, some pass drops, and on certain occasions, lining up over and defeating a tight end who is trying to block him.

Probably the most demanding of the unique positions in the Eagle is that of "B" linebacker, or the linebacker who aligns over the tight end. He has to have the ability to defeat the tight end, who is trying to block him or cover him man-for-man, as well as the ability to blitz or play zone pass coverage. These are difficult tasks, to say the least, and demand a special kind of player to perform them well.

Offensive football at all levels has become more and more wide open. By this I mean that offenses have forced the defense to defend the whole field on every down. There seems to be less emphasis on the power aspects of the game and more and more outside or perimeter running and passing. And if speed, quickness, and running ability are essential defensive qualities to defend against these offensive maneuvers, then it makes sense to put on the field as many defensive players as possible who possess these athletic skills. Thus the five-linebacker Eagle defense.

Of course, there are many different types of defensive schemes, and there seems to be no one philosophy whose implementation guarantees success. For example, for many years I have used a scheme that is basically conservative in nature. It was a bend-but-don't-break mode of defense. Although it was very successful, it was based on not giving up the big play; by its very nature it did not create opportunities for big plays by the defense. For the most part, the offense was able to predict the alignment and pass coverages, which meant the defense was reacting to the offense. However, using the multiple scheme and employing the bend-but-don't-break system in conjunction with the attacking schemes of the Eagle, has resulted in more pressure being put on the offensive team. Again, variety reduces predictability. Variety is much more effective when it includes the attacking and more conservative types of schemes.

This book lays a foundation for understanding the critical areas in teaching the Eagle defense, discussing the physical and mental qualifications for each position. It also covers the alignment for each position, along with the stance each player should use. It discusses the responsibilities and assignments for each position, along with the techniques necessary to play each position well.

The Hawk defensive variation is covered in Chapter 8, which discusses this unique alignment in detail. Covered are not only the positions that are different from the Eagle defense, but also those areas that are similar.

No book on technical football that I write would be complete without a thorough discussion of techniques and the drills to teach them. Coaching points for each position are a prominent part of this book. There is a progression of drills that moves from the most fundamental individual ones, to segment or group, to those involving the team.

Finally, pass coverages that fit the scheme along with dogs and blitzes are described in detail.

It has been a very long time since anything so revolutionary as the five-linebacker Eagle defense has been introduced at any level of football. It not only represents something unique, but its practical application to football today is documented.

This book is about a specific defensive scheme. However, the principles discussed in this book are applicable to the development and refinement of any type of alignment.

After reading this book, coaches at any level of football should be stimulated to think in terms of all the factors needed to develop and teach effective defense.

2

Bend But Don't Break

The 34 defense we have played for many years is the epitome of the bend-but-don't-break theory. It has as its roots patience, balance, simplicity, and efficiency. It is a balanced seven-man front. Three-deep zone is the most frequent pass coverage used. There is very little use of man-for-man coverage or of stunts and blitzes. Due to its design, there is a minimum of exposure to a big play by the offense. The theory is that the defense will limit the offense to minimum gains. We always say that if the offense is going to score, make them put together a 15-play drive to do it. This is in the belief that not too many offensive teams are capable of that kind of efficiency very many times during a ball game. Nor are there many coaches who are willing to develop a plan to attack a defense with the patience required to be successful against this type of defensive scheme.

The three linemen are two-gappers. That is, they line up head up on the tackles and center, knock them back, and are responsible for the gap to the side of the play. For example, the center is responsible for the "A" gap to his right or left. An occasional line slant is used to change up the line charge. The tackles are aligned in an outside shoulders alignment whenever a "rush" call is made. This alignment places them in a better position to rush the passer on passing downs. Since the type of defensive linemen we had were better suited to this type of defense, we committed ourselves to this style of play. Although our linemen were very good, strong players,

DIAGRAM 2–1
34 Defensive Alignment

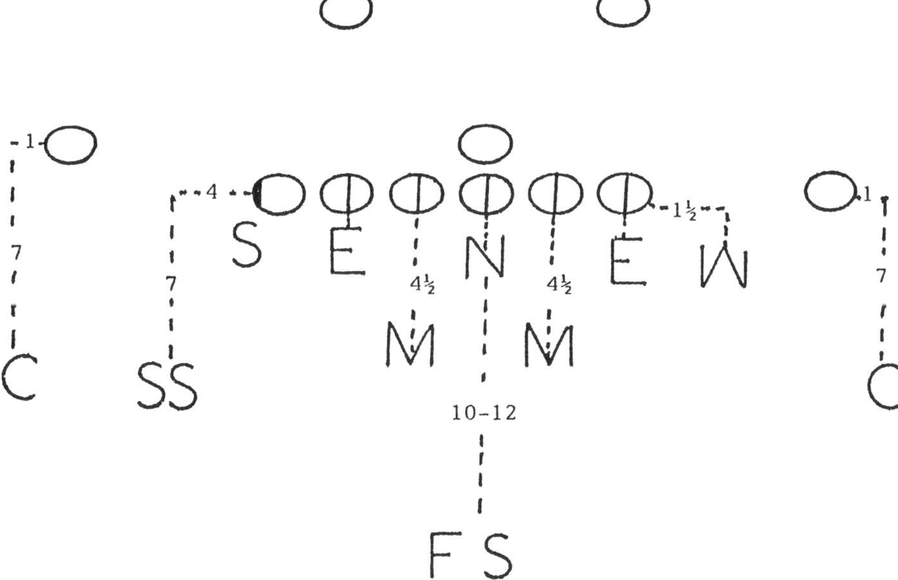

Alignments

Sam Linebacker – Outside shoulder of tight end.

Will Linebacker – 1½ yards outside offensive tackle on line of scrimmage.

Ends – Head up on offensive tackles. Note: May line up on outside shoulder of tackle when a rush call is made.

Nose – Head up on offensive center.

Mac Linebacker – Linebacker on tight end side lines up 4-4½ yards from the line of scrimmage head up offensive guard.

Mike Linebacker – Linebacker on the side opposite the tight end lines up 4-4½ yards from the line of scrimmage head up on the offensive guard.

Strong safety – 4 yards outside the tight end 7 yards from the line of scrimmage.

Free safety – 10-12 yards deep over the offensive center.

Corners – One yard outside the wide receiver seven yards from the line of scrimmage. May move to inside shoulder alignment on receiver when he aligns within five yards of the sideline.

they lacked the type of speed and quickness that is so essential in other types of defenses where they play wide or in the gaps.

We developed a style of defense to utilize the players we had. Although we were always looking for the quicker, faster type of linemen, we never seemed to be able to acquire or develop any. As a result, the system seemed to perpetuate itself; we continued to acquire and develop the same type of linemen—two-gappers.

Tied in very closely with the way the defensive linemen execute their responsibilities is the play of the inside linebackers. From their alignment 4 to $4\frac{1}{2}$ yards off the ball, they are expected to attack their base gap responsibility downhill or toward the line of scrimmage on all running plays. They are expected to make adjustments in their gap responsibilities according to the play of the defensive linemen. For example, if on a specific running play their gap responsibility is the "B" gap but the tackle on his side loses his "C" gap, the inside linebacker must make the adjustment. The fact that the tackle is hooked and ends up in the "B" gap means that the inside linebacker has the burden to adjust and assume responsibility for the "C" gap.

Since most of the pass coverages used in our 34 defense are of the zone variety, the inside linebackers are hook-to-curl pass defenders. Their specific responsibilities require them to limit the gain on balls thrown in the short zones. If they can read patterns well and react with a high degree of velocity to the look and throw of the quarterback, the inside linebackers can determine, by their play, whether or not a team can play zone pass defense successfully.

The outside linebackers must be able to defeat a tight end's one-on-one block. They must also be able to close the off-tackle hole and defeat blocks by linemen and running backs. Their primary roles in the pass defense are as outside pass rushers and flat defenders. They are most effective when they rush on the open side of the formation. There is no question that these two players are the most effective pass rushers in this scheme. This is due to two factors: their physical makeup and the fact that they are committed as outside pass rushers by coverage designs.

In our 34 defense, we have made very little distinction between the free safety and strong safety positions. This is due primarily to the fact that we want to roll or rotate our safeties when change-of-strength motion by the offense occurs. And although this requires both safeties to learn the technique and responsibilities inherent in the free and strong safety positions, it does allow much smoother adjustment to motion. Generally speaking, the free safety is more of a pass coverage type of player and the strong safety is best equipped in size and temperament to be a run forcer. Safeties in our scheme are generally run forcers against the run, especially on the strong side where we like to play safety force most of the time.

They are generally responsible for the deep middle one-third zone as a free safety and a curl-to-flat defender as a strong safety. In man-for-man coverage, the free safety is a deep middle one-third zone defender, and the strong safety is usually responsible for man coverage. He covers the tight end or inside receiver in a slot formation man for man.

The corners in our 34 defense are primarily zone pass defenders responsible for the deep outside one-third zones. Occasionally, they are flat defenders when we roll the zone their way. We do ask our corners to be run forcers in some coverages. And although we prefer safety force in our 34 scheme, minimum splits by receivers do cause us to have to use corner forces.

To summarize, our 34 defense is a conservative system—a bend-but-don't-break style of play. The linemen are two-gappers whose basic job is to knock back the linemen they line up over. This allows the inside linebackers to move freely up and in and go get the ball carrier. It is based on positive gap control, meaning a defensive player is responsible for each gap on every running play. The tight-end-side outside linebacker's job is to defeat the tight end. The linebacker on the side opposite the tight end has, as his major job, rushing the passer. Zone is the basic coverage used, and the secondary players are expected to be good zone pass defenders as well as run forcers. Our 34 defense is a conservative, sound system that has been very successful in accomplishing what we attempted to do with it. For many years, it was the best thing we could do within the framework of the personnel we had. The areas where it fell short were lack of creating big-play opportunities for our defense, turnovers, and pressure on the quarterback.

NICKEL 40 DEFENSE
(Diagram 2–2)

Initially in our nickel defense, we used four defensive linemen, two linebackers, and five defensive backs. However, as the offensive teams began to use more wide receivers and fewer running backs, it made sense to use more defensive backs in the game. We began to use six defensive backs, and at times we now use seven against some teams. We also changed our thinking on the four pass rushers in the nickel defense. In an attempt to get more speed and quickness on the field, we now use outside linebackers as defensive ends or outside pass rushers. By doing this, we are using players who are accustomed to rushing the passer from the outside position in our base defense. This means they have additional opportunities to use skills they have acquired, and at the same time we give them more chances to develop skills in practice. We tried for several years to use

DIAGRAM 2–2
Nickel 40 Alignment

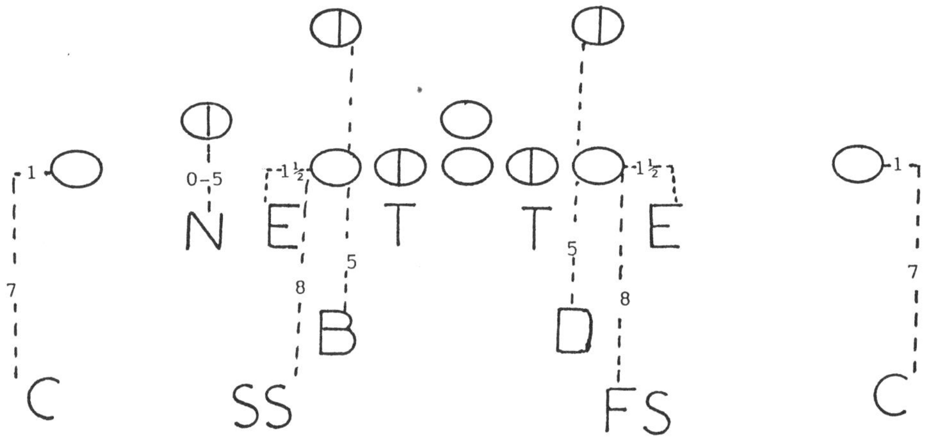

Ends – One to one-and-a-half yards outside offensive tackle.

Tackles – Head up to outside shoulder of offensive guard.

Backer – Inside shoulder on back your side five yards from line of scrimmage.

Dime – Inside shoulder on back your side five yards from line of scrimmage.

Nickel – Head up to inside eye of #2 receiver strongside. Vary alignment from on the line of scrimmage to five yards from line of scrimmage.

Safeties – Outside shoulder of offensive tackle eight yards from the line of scrimmage.

Corners – One yard outside wide receiver your side, seven yards from the line of scrimmage. Apply sideline rule and line up inside shoulder alignment on receiver when he aligns within five yards of the sideline.

the two-gap type of lineman as a pass rusher only to find he was not equipped well enough athletically in the areas of speed and quickness to be effective. The defensive tackles in our nickel defense have been the two-gap linemen in our 34 defense. They are physically best equipped as inside rushers. However, we have now replaced one of them with a linebacker to give us more quickness and speed in an inside rush position.

DIAGRAM 2–3
Nickel 33 Alignment

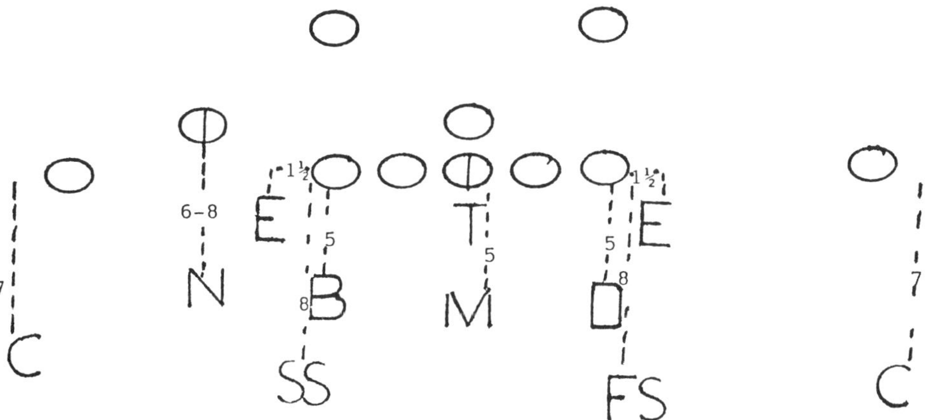

Mac linebacker replaces defensive tackle - controls nose tackle rush by call - Mac is a pass rusher on all normal nickel coverages. Backer or dime can be used as rushers and Mac replaces the rusher and assumes his coverage.

NICKEL 33 DEFENSE
(Diagram 2–3)

The utilization of a linebacker at one of the defensive tackle positions has another advantage for us. This allows us to move or stem him back to a linebacker position, which means we now have the ability to move from a four-man to a three-man rush defense or vice versa. The other tackle moves head up on the center, and this gives us an odd defense to go along with the even. It also allows us to use eight pass defenders in some coverages, which we think is a very valuable tool against some types of offensive schemes. The outside pass rushers' and all of the pass defenders' responsibilities remain the same as they were in the four-down linemen defense. This means that the nose tackle and the linebacker who replaces the other tackle are the only really new positions in this nickel 33 defense. There are endless possibilities in the way of stunts between the middle linebacker, the linemen, and the defensive backs. Again, this type of versatility is effective in creating uncertainty in the offense, yet it does not involve vast amounts of new learning.

The foundations of our Eagle defense are inherent in the defensive schemes that have been described in this chapter. Although the Eagle is much different in design than our 34 scheme, we tried to incorporate as many of our defensive principles as we could. We also tried to standardize, as much as possible, the responsibilities of the various players that we were asking to play multiple positions in the various alignments.

3

The Need to Attack

Modern-day offensive football is characterized by an increasing emphasis on the forward pass at all levels of competition. Although teams have always passed to some extent on first and second downs, the frequency of passing in these situations is increasing at a rapid rate. One of the ways in which defensive teams must defend the pass is to be able to generate an effective pass rush. The key here is to be able to pass rush without having to blitz or dog linebackers on a regular basis. When defensive teams have to do this, they are exposed to big plays by the offense. In my opinion, the best way to rush the passer in these situations is to, by defensive design, put as many players as possible in advantageous rush positions by their alignment, assignment, and techniques. When this is done, a defensive team is able to put pressure on the passer and maintain the ability to play these base pass coverages without having to dog or blitz.

The most effective way for an interior lineman to rush the passer is in the gaps between the offensive linemen. This position allows a rusher to get on the corners of a blocker quickly and increases his chances of beating him. When a player is lined up head up or in a two-gap position on an offensive lineman, he is in a disadvantageous position to rush the passer. This is due to the fact that he has to control the blockers before he can work on the corners of the man. This takes valuable time and gives the advantage to the offensive man. When he is in a gap or lined up on the corner of the blocker, the advantage is with the defensive man.

The problem with two-gap players becoming pass rushers is that the teaching of the technique requires a lot of practice time. To lead with the hands, defeat the blocker, read the blocking scheme, and defend the play-side gap is very time consuming. When a team uses a two-gap scheme on a regular basis, there is not much practice time left for pass rush. When we were exclusively a two-gap team on early downs, the only time we worked on pass rush was when we practiced our nickel defense.

Our problem was to find ways to create an environment where we would be able to develop pass rushers out of our 34 defensive linemen. The first step was to develop the Eagle schemes that allowed the linemen to line up in the gap between the guard and tackle and penetrate on pass rush. Obviously, by utilizing this scheme we created situations in practice where defensive linemen rushed the passer over and over again, without the burden of first having to knock back a lineman before he rushed the passer. We found that men who were not very good in the area could become effective.

Even though our outside linebackers were not real productive pass rushers in the 34 defense, they were, by their athletic ability, potentially our best pass rushers. The problem here was to find the most advantageous alignment to put them in.

In our 34 defense, the linebacker on the open or split side of the formation has been the most effective pass rusher. This is due to the fact that he rushes on air, or without an offensive lineman lined up in front of him. This allows him to gain velocity and adjust his angles as he rushes the passer. The fact that he does not have to be concerned about as many types of run threats as the strongside linebacker also contributes to his effectiveness as a rusher.

We therefore created alignments for our outside linebackers where they lined up wide. We want them lined up at least 1½ yards outside the nearest offensive lineman on the line of scrimmage. Their base job is to rush the passer on every down. We did not want to complicate their assignments with multiple techniques and styles of play. Their job is to rush the passer and react to the run.

In this scheme it is critical that both tackles and both outside linebackers understand that their primary job is to rush the passer. They are penetrators who read and react to blocking schemes and play patterns as they attack the offense.

The nose linebacker is not a static player in this scheme. He is—in all man coverages, dogs, and blitzes—a mover or penetrator. Although he is aligned in a head-up position on the center on the snap, he is penetrating a gap or executing a game or stunt with a tackle on every play.

Although a lineman may also be used in this position, we feel this defense has the most flexibility when it uses a linebacker in this position. If a lineman is used, he can be used to two-gap as well as to game and stunt. However, with a lineman in the nose position the defense loses the flexibility of having the nose available as a pass dropper in zone coverage.

It is important that the job description be the same whether the nose man is a lineman or linebacker. The job has to be to rush the passer and react to the run if the defense is to be as effective as it can be.

A BETTER WAY TO DOG OR BLITZ

The 34 defense does not lend itself well to dogging or blitzing. The fact that the linemen and inside linebackers line up head up on offensive players is a limiting factor. It is relatively simple for offensive teams to block linemen and linebackers who dog and blitz from those head-up alignments. And although it is possible to move players in the gaps, there is a loss of effectiveness when a defense reveals its intent by assuming these alignments.

The Eagle defense, by its design, uses five players to rush the passer on every down. It also has three other players—the linebacker over the tight end, the Mac linebacker, and the strong safety—who line up on or within five yards of the line of scrimmage. This means that they are in advantageous positions to dog or blitz. The relative positions of players in this defense, along with the penetrating, pass-rushing philosophy of the scheme, make it a very effective way to pressure offensive teams.

The Eagle defense grew out of a definite need to develop a pass rush on first and second downs. It is our way of creating an environment in which to rush the passer and defend the run with an aggressive, penetrating style of defense. It represents our response to a definite need. I think one of the most critical factors in coaching is the ability to take the personnel at hand and develop ways to make them more effective players. This unique defensive scheme does exactly that.

4

Eagle Defense Symbols and Alignments

Defensive football is, for the most part, reaction or adjustment to the offensive team. Therefore, before a defensive scheme can be implemented and understood, it is necessary to establish terminology and designations as they relate to offensive formations. These will also serve as forms of reference as you become familiar with the Eagle defense. Diagrams 4–1 and 4–2 present the Eagle defense symbols and alignment for run gaps, pass defense zones, and receiver designations.

RUN GAPS

For the purpose of communication, the gaps, or areas between the offensive linemen, are labeled by a letter. These gaps move as the offensive personnel move after the ball is snapped and the running play develops. If a defensive team's design is sound, each gap is the specific responsibility of a specific player on every running play. In some schemes like the 34 defense, the linemen are responsible for two gaps. This is usually the case when linemen are lined up head on the offensive lineman. For example, in many 34 schemes, the nose tackle is a "two-gapper." That is, he is responsible for both of the gaps on either side of the center. Which one of these he is responsible for is determined by the play run by the offense. If,

DIAGRAM 4–1
Eagle Defense Symbols and Alignment

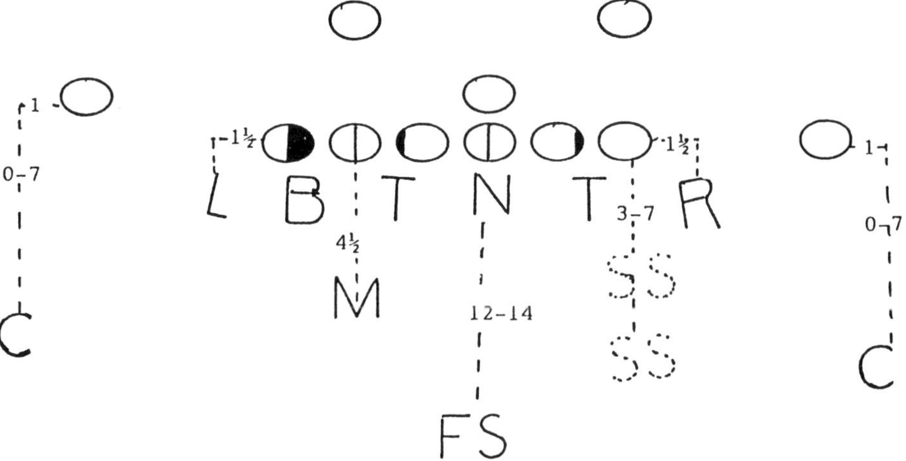


```
L  - Left outside linebacker
R  - Right outside linebacker
T  - Right and left tackle
N  - Nose linebacker
M  - Mac linebacker
B  - Linebacker who lines up over the tight end
SS - Strong safety-alignment within five yards of the line
of scrimmage makes the defense an eight-man front
FS - Free safety - deep middle third defender most coverages
C  - Corners - outside deep defenders who are lined up
over wide receivers most coverages
```

for example, the design of the play is to run the ball to the right of the center, the nose is responsible for the gap between the center and guard to the right. If the play is designed to go to the left of the center, then his gap is to his left.

Since the Eagle is a penetrating type of defense, we try to keep our players out of two-gap assignments as much as possible.

Gap Designations

"A" Gap—Between the center and guard.

"B" Gap—Between the guard and tackle.

DIAGRAM 4–2
Run Gaps—Receiver Designations—Pass Zones

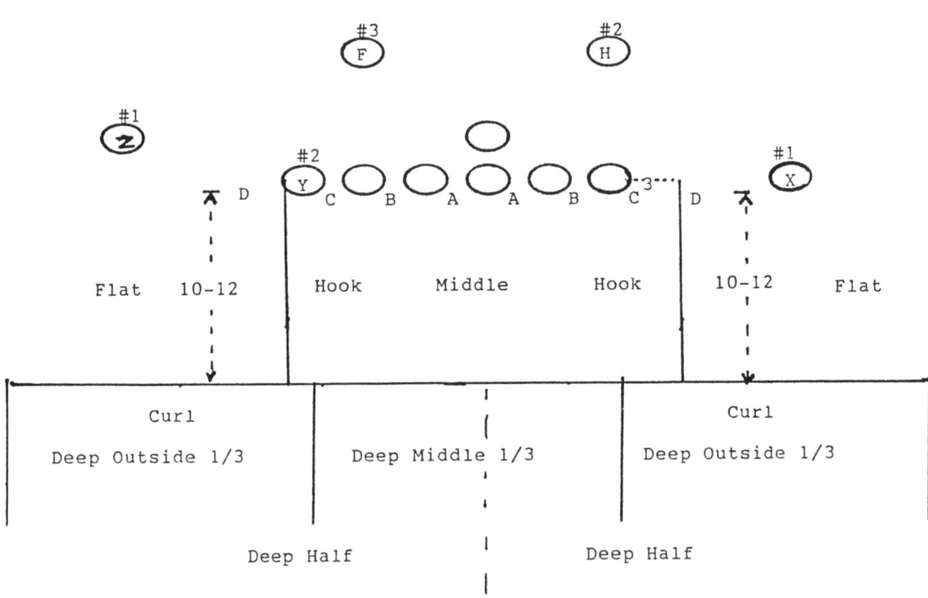

"C" Gap—Between the tackle and tight end; outside the tackle on the side where there is no tight end.

"D" Gap—Outside the tight end or the wide outside area on the side where there is no tight end.

PASS DEFENSE ZONES

In zone pass coverage, the field is divided into zones or areas that become the responsibility of a specific pass defender. They vary in width and depth and are defined in more specific terms according to offensive formations. These zones are overlapping and when they become the responsibility of a pass defender, they should be described accordingly. For example, a short inside zone pass defender is called a hook defender. In the Eagle defense, the Mac linebacker is the strongside hook defender. However, depending on the pattern run and the direction in which the quarterback is looking, he is expected to defend the curl area as well. Therefore, the specific zone responsibility of the Mac linebacker should be described as that of hook-to-curl defender. When a flat or outside defender is an outside linebacker or safety, his responsibility should be described as curl to flat. This means it is his responsibility to hold off or defend the pass in the curl area until the hook defender can get there. If the flat defender is a cornerback, his responsibility should be described as flat to curl. This means that as the cornerback rolls up to jam the wide receiver, with no flat threat he can collapse to the curl area. This overlapping of the underneath or designated zones is a principle that is absolutely essential for the short defender to understand if he is to be effective in executing his responsibilities.

Vertically, the pass defense zones are defined in terms of distance from the line of scrimmage. The general categories of these areas are the short and deep zones. The area between the short and deep zones is called the intermediate area. This intermediate area ties together the short and deep zones. These vertical zones, like the horizontal zones, overlap. Players responsible for short zones must understand when it is their responsibility to carry receivers through the intermediate areas. Similarly, it is critical that deep defenders understand that specific pass routes and pass patterns, along with the quarterback's look and throw, will dictate that they must make plays on thrown balls in the intermediate as well as the deep zones.

Zones Defined

Flat Zones—Short, outside zones that extend vertically from the line of scrimmage to approximately 10 to 12 yards deep. Horizontally, they start at the outside edge of the yard-line numbers on an NFL field and extend to the sideline.

Hook Zones—Short, inside zones that extend vertically from the line of scrimmage to a depth of approximately 10 to 12 yards deep. Horizontally, they extend from slightly outside the tight-end position to about the middle of the offensive formation.

Middle Area—The area between the hook zones; it extends vertically 10 to 12 yards deep.

Curl Zones—The areas between the hook and flat zones that extend from the line of scrimmage to a depth of anywhere from 15 to 25 yards deep. Horizontally, they start at the yard-line numbers on an NFL field and extend in approximately five yards.

Deep Zones

In three-deep zone defenses, the field is divided into thirds or three deep zones. These zones extend vertically from approximately 12 yards from the line of scrimmage to the opponent's goal line. Laterally or horizontally, the deep zones are approximately 18 yards wide. The two outside zones are the deep outside, and the zone between them is the deep middle.

In the two-deep type of zone coverage, the field is divided into halves horizontally. Due to the fact that two-deep defenders are each responsible for zones that are about 27 yards wide, their areas of responsibility start deeper, at about 15 yards from the line of scrimmage.

RECEIVER DESIGNATIONS

In order to establish the best possible means by which defensive players and coaches can communicate, a system of receiver designation must be established. This is usually done with letters or numbers. Although I have always used letters to designate these offensive players, a system of numbers is easier to understand. I prefer using both letters and numbers, the letters for brevity and the numbers for simplicity.

Strongside Receivers

Z—Is the number-one or the outside receiver on the strong side.

Y—Is the number-two receiver on the strong side, counting from the outside in. The tight end in a regular formation or the inside receiver in a slot formation is the Y.

F—Is the number-three receiver on the strong side. A back in the fullback position in a regular formation is an F or number-three receiver strongside. The tight end in a trips formation is another example of a number-three strongside or F receiver.

Weakside Receivers

X—Is the number-one or outside receiver on the weak side of the formation. In a slot formation, the tight end is the X receiver.

H—Is the number-two or inside receiver on the weak side of the formation. Usually a back occupies this position. In a one-back formation, the H can be a back, but it can also be a tight end.

The information in this chapter is meant to assist you in understanding the terms and forms of reference I use in the remainder of the book. It also allows me to use the abbreviated terms described above.

5

The Front Six

This chapter discusses the front six positions in the Eagle defense—the outside linebackers; the tackles; the linebacker who plays over the tight end; and the nose linebacker, who plays over the center—in detail. It describes the physical and mental requirements for these positions, as well as the alignment, stance, and responsibilities of each. Diagram 5–1 illustrates the alignment of the front six in the Eagle defense.

OUTSIDE LINEBACKERS

The primary responsibility of the outside linebackers in the Eagle defense is to rush the passer. They are pass rushers first and run reactors second. That is, they should not be slowed down in their pass rush by their concern for run responsibilities.

DIAGRAM 5–1
Eagle Defense: The Front Six

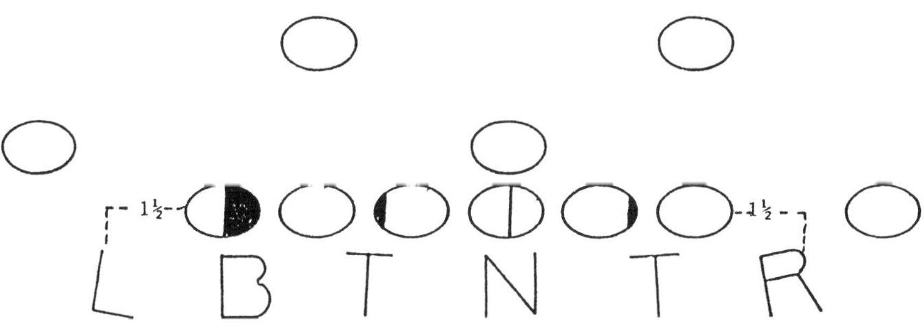

Physical Qualifications

Quickness and Speed

The most important physical qualities for an outside linebacker are quickness and speed. Initial quickness is really the most critical of these attributes. Takeoff, or reaction to the movement of the ball and the offensive man, is a natural part of the player's makeup, but there is no doubt this can be improved with work. In fact, over the years, I believe I have seen more improvement in initial quickness than in any other physical skill. Repetitive takeoff drills are the best way to accomplish this.

Speed, or the ability to run well, enables the player to get from one point to the other quickly. The outside linebacker who can run is able to put constant pressure on the passer, make plays on perimeter runs, and chase down plays going away from him. Although speed is an innate quality, it can be improved with work on the start (or takeoff), on balance, and on the technique of running.

Strength

Strength is important to an outside linebacker because it enables him to take on and defeat blockers, especially in the running game. The strength we are most concerned with is what I call explosive strength. That is, the player has the ability to defeat blockers on the run or while he is moving. Strength in the hands, arms, and back is probably the most critical at this position. It is, however, an asset to have players who have good lower body strength as well. This, of course, enables them to be better equipped to defeat the bigger offensive players when it is necessary to do so.

Change of Direction

Along with speed and quickness, the ability to change directions is very high on the list of the physical qualifications necessary to play the outside linebacker positions well. The players who can execute this skill best are the ones who can play with their weight distributed over the balls of their feet. They are the players who possess good bend, or flexion, at their ankles, knees, and hips. This type of weight distribution allows players to always be in a position to change directions and react quickly to what they see. This is especially essential to outside linebackers who are in the continual process of rushing the passer but must react to running plays. This skill can be improved with repetitive drill work. Any type of drill that requires players to change directions quickly, like wave drills or over-dummy movement drills, will improve players' abilities in this area.

Pass Rush

Although players must be taught the techniques required to rush the passer effectively, it is true that some innately possess this skill to a greater degree than others. In selecting players to play this position, it is crucial to select those who are the best natural pass rushers on the team.

Instincts

The outside linebackers are big-play makers in the defense. Obviously, the more a player possesses an instinctive or natural ability to make plays against the run or pass, the more successful he will be in playing this position. Again, when players are selected as outside linebackers, they must be the type who have the greatest capacity for making big defensive plays on a regular basis.

Mental Qualifications

The outside linebacker position is not a demanding position mentally. There are not very many different assignments he is asked to execute. His job is to rush the passer and react to the run on every play. Because his assignments are not complex or mentally demanding, he should be able to play with great velocity without being slowed down by the mental processes.

Alignment

It is important that the outside linebackers line up wide. Their outside alignment not only puts them in the most advantageous pass rush position, it also allows them time to adjust and react to running plays. The linebacker on the tight-end side lines up 1½ yards outside the tight end on the line of scrimmage. The open side, or the linebacker away from the tight end, lines up 1½ yards outside the offensive tackle. These are the base alignments. They may vary by game or stunt, down and distance, formation, score, and time left in a game. It is important to note that most adjustments will be made to a wider, rather than a tighter, alignment. Again, width in alignment is absolutely essential to the proper execution of their responsibilities by the outside linebackers. Generally, wider alignments are used as adjustments for better pass rush angles and run force angles over flexed tight ends or wingbacks lined up tight. Tighter alignments are used only in order for the outside linebackers to better execute a game or stunt that takes them to an inside gap.

Stance

Either an up or down stance may be used by the outside linebacker. There are advantages to both types of stances. Generally, the up position places a player in a better position to be able to see and adjust to blockers, especially those assigned to block them using pre-snap motion. The three-point stance, or down position, enables the player to exercise better takeoff, or quicker reaction and acceleration to the snap or to movement by an offensive player. Each one of these stances has its advantages and therefore disadvantages. Without question, I think that the up position is the best stance for a player whose background is that of an outside linebacker and who is obviously more comfortable playing up. If, however, a defensive lineman is being trained to play the position, it may be prudent to allow him to use a three-point stance.

The up stance consists of the player at about a 45-degree angle, lining up on the line of scrimmage, turned in, with his outside foot back. He should have good body lean, with his weight distributed over the balls of his feet and good flexion at the ankles, knees, and hips. His front foot should be pointed in at about a 45-degree angle with the back foot pointed out at about an angle that will give him a wide surface to push off from. It is important that the player be able to roll off the front foot as well as push off the back foot. This is accomplished by exaggerating the bend in the front leg, thus increasing the body lean. With the weight distributed over the front foot and with body lean, the player is assured that his movement at the snap will be more upfield, or across the line of scrimmage. This type of stance also allows the player consistent, sure footing and decreases his chances of slipping, as happens when the player is in a more upright stance and merely pushes off his back foot.

The three-point stance, or the down position, can be likened to the sprinter's stance in the starting blocks. As in the up position, the player should be lined up pointing in to better see the ball and any player movement. This stance also enables him to attack at an angle to close the inside angles. It is an elongated stance with a good deal of the player's weight on the hand he has on the ground. He should be up on the balls of his feet with weight distributed equally on them. Again, equal weight distribution here prevents the slipping that occurs when there is too much pressure placed on the back foot. This stance may be altered somewhat when the player's responsibilities are changed by a game or stunt. It is, however, important to point out that the success of this scheme is dependent upon the two outside linebackers attacking the offense with great velocity on a regular basis. Any attempt to change their style of play should be done only with a great deal of thought.

Regardless of the type of stance used, it is important that these players be coached to take off and attack upfield. All their movement should be, as much as possible, across the line of scrimmage.

Responsibilities

The primary responsibilities of the outside linebackers are to rush the passer and react to the run. It is very important that they be coached to think in terms of sprinting across the line of scrimmage and reacting on the run rather than sitting on the line of scrimmage and reading. They are outside, or contain, rushers, but they should be allowed to make inside pass rush moves when the opportunity presents itself.

When running plays develop to their side of the formation, it is the responsibility of the outside linebackers to contain, force, or turn the play in. However, there are occasions when the ball is attacking the perimeter that it is permissible for an outside linebacker to "bounce" the ball carrier outside, provided he is forced to do it at a depth of two to three yards in the offensive backfield. On running plays designed to go to the opposite side, the outside linebacker is responsible for reverses and wide cutbacks. However, he must be coached to adjust his pursuit angles to be an active playmaker on all runs to the opposite side of the line of scrimmage.

Techniques

Reaction to movement, or takeoff, is where it all starts for the outside linebackers. Their effectiveness as attackers is dependent upon their ability to explode or sprint across the line of scrimmage on the snap.

The aiming point for the player is a spot about four yards deep behind the center (the position of a fullback's alignment in a normal formation).

Run

On the snap, the outside linebacker sprints across the line of scrimmage. His initial path should be to the spot just described. As he attacks, he should read the near back and pulling lane. It is important that he see this area, since his reaction depends on the activity there. The near back is the closest back to him in the offensive formation. The pulling lane is that area immediately behind the offensive line of scrimmage where pulling linemen appear when they are assigned to block players on the defensive perimeter. The outside linebacker will take on and defeat all blockers that come to block him from the inside with his hands or inside arm. Although the technique we want is aggressive—come after the offense and make things happen on their side of the line of scrimmage— we do not want them taking on blockers from the inside with their outside arm. This wrong-shoulder technique is not acceptable because it allows a blocker to take a defender out of the play and eliminates him as a possible tackler. The only time when this technique is permissible is when an outside linebacker reads a gap or counter OT play quickly and his quick reaction allows him to occupy both the tackle and guard pulling from the opposite side of the formation. It is important that the player be coached to close the off-tackle hole with the blockers blocking him with techniques that will force the football deeper and wider than the design of the play. When this happens, the fact that he is playing with his outside arm and leg free should allow him to accelerate off the blocker and make the tackle on the ball carrier. It is really important to stress the pointed or turned-in aspects of the stance since this should establish a path or route that will allow him to squeeze or tighten the inside lanes. If his angle is too much upfield, it is difficult to be able to compress these off-tackle running lanes.

Pass

Velocity, or speed, best describes the general types of pass rushes used by the outside linebackers. Their wide outside alignment does put additional pressure on the offensive players assigned to block them. Since distance is a factor here, it is important that all pass rush moves and techniques be based on the player's sprinting across the line of scrimmage to actually beat the offensive player to the junction, or the point where he is going to attempt to block him.

It all starts with good takeoff, or explosion, across the line of scrimmage on the snap. There are two basic types of pass rush used by these players. They are: a hard outside rush around the outside corner of the blocker—or the counter to this, which is a hard upfield outside rush accompanied by an inside or underneath move on the blocker.

The hard outside move involves the defensive man sprinting through the junction where the offensive lineman is expecting to block him. The less contact with the blocker, the better. However, there are very few times when the defensive man will be able to run by the blockers and sack the quarterback without first having to defeat him. The technique should start with the rusher reaching with his outside arm and grabbing the outside arm or shoulder pad of the blocker. At the same time, the right arm of the rusher should be used in a ripping action. As an alternate technique, a swim or arm-over technique with the inside arm may be used. Once the rusher is past the blocker, he should strive to keep his path, or angle of rush, as close as possible to a direct path or shortest possible route to the passer. If the quarterback steps up, it is important that the rusher reach around for the passer with the outside arm. This reach-around technique should be accompanied by the toe of the rusher pointing back toward the line of scrimmage. The attempt here is to get the rusher moving back toward the quarterback as he moves forward in the pocket.

The counter to the hard upfield rush is the inside move on the blocker. The technique begins with the rusher threatening to beat the block outside. After five or more steps are taken up the field or when the rusher's head is upfield as far as the outside shoulder of the blocker, the inside move is made. The threat of the hard outside rush must force the blocker to turn toward the defensive man as he sets to block him. This should cause the blocker to establish a relationship with the line of scrimmage where his shoulders are perpendicular, thereby reducing his chances to recover and to effectively block the rusher making the inside move.

After the rusher has established his upfield position and the blocker has turned, the rusher should, under control, club or pull the inside arm or shoulder of the blocker and at the same time, rip or swim with the outside arm as he goes by the blocker on his move to the quarterback.

If the blocker sets too deep or too soft, attempting to adjust his pass-blocking set to the outside rush or outside rush counter, it is advisable to leverage or power-rush over the blocker. This technique is executed with the rusher driving his hands at the blocker, aiming to make contact at the tips of the numbers or under the shoulder pads of the blocker. The blow is struck with the palms and heels to extend or lock out his arms at the elbows and at the same time, roll his hips or involve the big muscles with good bend at the ankles, knees, and hips. It is important that the rusher keep his shoulder level lower than that of the blocker as this ensures that he will be in a leverage or power position that is better than the blocker's. This technique is used to defeat the blocker by either driving him back into the passer or accelerating off him and then attacking the passer.

The specific pass blockers the outside linebacker must defeat are the offensive tackles, the tight end, the offensive guard, or the running back. Which player will be assigned to block the outside linebacker is determined by the pass-blocking schemes of the offensive team. The tackle will be assigned to block the outside linebacker more frequently than any other offensive player. He is usually the most difficult for the linebacker to defeat due to two basic factors—the size differential and the proximity of the tackle to the rusher, which seem to work in favor of the offensive tackle. More than any other skill, takeoff and speed are the skills the rusher must use to his advantage over this specific player.

On the strong side of the formation, the tight end is occasionally used to block the outside linebacker on pass plays. This player is usually the least effective in pass blocking an outside linebacker. The reason for this is that tight ends do not spend much time practicing pass blocking. Most of their practice time is spent developing run-blocking and pass-receiving skills. Therefore, it is reasonable to expect that, when this mismatch occurs, the defensive player will win.

Running backs are accustomed to blocking outside linebackers in pass protection with various types of drop-back and play-action pass schemes. When this situation presents itself, we expect the linebacker to win these battles every time. This is due to the fact that the back is at a great disadvantage because the defensive man has generated such a high degree of velocity. This, coupled with the fact that there is usually a great physical advantage, means the rusher should be able to combine these two factors and run through the blocker to the passer.

This is the technique I described earlier in this chapter. The counter to this power, or leverage, move is to approach the blocker as if the plan was to power rush over him, force the blocker to brace or set for the contact, and then make either the outside or inside move on him.

Occasionally, the guard will be asked to block the outside rushers on pass plays. Although this does not occur frequently, when it does it should mean a win for the defense. Again, takeoff and speed are important because the offensive player is at a disadvantage due to the fact that he has to move so far to get to a junction point to block the rusher. This is especially true on the tight-end side of the formation where the distance the guard has to travel to block is greater.

TACKLES

Like the outside linebackers, the tackles in the Eagle defense are pass rushers and run reactors. They are not required to play a lot of different ways. Their position is not complicated by multiple assignments. It does not take a specific body type to play the position well. Virtually any type of lineman, well coached and motivated, can be successful as a defensive tackle. The player can bring varying degrees of speed, size, and strength to the position but will not be hampered in his ability to achieve by limitations in any of these areas.

Physical Qualifications

Quickness

Initial quickness, or the ability to quickly gain ground upfield on the snap, is the most important of the physical qualifications of a tackle. This is a skill that can be improved with practice. In fact, if the player understands how important initial quickness is to playing this position, practice will serve as opportunity to improve.

Strength

Since the tackles are required to defeat the blocks of offensive linemen, it is important that they have good strength in their hands and arms as well as their lower bodies. Again, explosive strength is what we want here. The ability to react quickly to the snap of the ball, the ability to hit and not have to stop or slow down to do it, are all part of "explosive strength."

Speed

Since speed is an essential factor in pass rush, it is an important skill for tackles to possess. The ability to run fast is also an asset to a tackle and is the most important factor in his ability to make plays in the running game, especially on plays that are run away from him.

Instincts

Instinctiveness is important to playing the tackle position well in the Eagle defense. A player with good instincts will react better and make more big plays than the one who is less gifted. Instincts allow a tackle to quickly sort through the helmets, arms, legs, and feet, and find the ball.

Change of Direction

The ability to change directions is important due to the penetrating nature of the position. When the tackle penetrates in the gap between the offensive guard or tackle he has to be able to react quickly and establish the quickest path to the ball. The player who can change directions will take short, direct routes and make plays on the ball. Individuals who cannot change directions well will react by taking rounded rather than straight-line paths to the ball and as a result, end up chasing ball carriers rather than tackling them.

Ability to Use Hands

The ability to use his hands to defeat a blocker is without question the most useful single physical skill a defensive player can possess. This technique can be developed and the ability to teach this skill well is without question the trademark of all really good defensive line coaches. The ability to execute the hands technique is more important in defensive schemes where the linemen line up in a two-gap or head-on position. In the Eagle defense, the tackles line up in gaps, and their penetration on the snap does not require them to lead with their hands as other schemes do. This technique does become important, however, after they have penetrated, when they need to be able to use their hands to ward off blockers and gain operating space to pursue to the ball or rush the passer.

Pass Rush

The tackles in the Eagle defense have as their basic responsibility rushing the passer. Therefore, the ability to be effective as pass rushers is important.

As inside pass rushers, these players need to be able to penetrate and work to pressure the quarterback in front of them. Speed and quickness are important qualities, but strength and the ability to use their hands, along with takeoff, are the more critical skills that determine success in this area.

Alignment

The tackles line up on the line of scrimmage in the gap between the guard and tackle. More specifically, their inside eye should be across from the tip of the outside shoulder of the guard. The width of this alignment may vary some and is usually affected by several factors. First, the width of the split of the guard from the center is important. If the split gets too wide by giving him too large an area to close inside, the tackle must move to a tighter shade on the guard. Another factor that may affect the way the tackle lines up is the split between the guard and tackle. Generally, he will line up tighter on the guard with a tight split. The wider the gap is, the wider he should line up. The run strength of a formation also affects the alignment of the tackles. Generally, with the run strength away from him, the tackle lines up tighter on the guard. Another factor that affects his alignment is the game or stunt or line charge variation he will be executing. The general rule is that he lines up in the best possible alignment to execute his responsibility. The tackle will line up tighter if he is going inside, and wider if he is going outside.

Down and distance can also affect alignment. On short yardage or run downs, a tighter alignment is more beneficial, while on passing downs, a wider position enhances his chance for effectiveness as a pass rusher.

Stance

An elongated three-point sprinter's stance, pointed in slightly, is the type best suited to the requirements of the tackle position. This stance enables him to explode upfield on his initial takeoff, penetrate, pass rush, and react to the run. It is best for the left tackle to use a right-handed stance or a stance with his right hand on the ground. This type of stance is beneficial since it affords him the opportunity to take his initial step with his right or inside foot and come to a relatively squared-up position. The right tackle should line up in a stance with his left hand down for the same reasons described above. If it is too difficult for a naturally right-handed player to learn to play effectively in a left-handed stance, it is wise to allow that player to use a right-handed stance. However, he will have to learn to play with what I call a step and a shuffle. In other words, he will have to learn to take a half-step with his inside leg to square up or balance up after his initial step with the outside leg.

In this elongated stance, the tackle should have a good deal of weight forward on his down hand. He should be up on the balls of his feet and on his initial movement have the feeling of pushing off his back foot and rolling off his front foot. It is important that he be turned in to better see the movement of the ball at the snap and also to play his base run responsibility, which is inside or the area between him and the nose.

Responsibility

The job of the tackle is to penetrate in the gap between the offensive guard and the tackle. He is an inside pass rusher and responsible for the "B" gap on running plays his way. On runs away from him, he is a chase man. That is, he is expected to pursue on the offensive side of the line of scrimmage and take a proper angle that will enable him to tackle the ball carrier. It is important that he perceive his job as to make things happen on the offensive side of the line of scrimmage.

The basic key for the tackle is the action of the offensive guard. He must see the guard and react to his actions. If the guard tries to block the tackle out, he must close or squeeze the gap. If the guard tries to reach-block, he must penetrate in the "B" gap. The takeoff of the tackle should ensure that he cannot be reached by the guard. If the guard pulls to the opposite side, the tackle should flatten his route and pursue at an angle to tackle the ball carrier. If the guard pulls to the outside, the tackle should flatten his route as quickly as possible and pressure with a good angle to the ball.

The penetration by the tackle should ensure that the offensive tackle cannot succeed in blocking him on any running plays. If both the guard and tackle block him, he must fight to hold the "B" gap with penetration.

On most passing plays, the offensive guard will be assigned to block the tackle. Therefore, it is the job of the tackle on passing plays to beat the guard with his pass rush technique. His responsibility is to beat the guard upfield and outside. If he cannot beat him outside, he should make an inside pass rush move on him.

Technique

On the snap, the tackle should sprint through the gap between the offensive guard and tackle. He is concerned with making things happen by penetrating and disrupting the blocking schemes on the offensive side of the line of scrimmage. It is important that the tackle concentrate on keeping his shoulder level down so that he is gaining as much distance as possible across the line of scrimmage. If he comes up and raises his shoulder, this will result in his playing too high, exposing too much blocking surface to the blockers, and reducing his ability to disrupt their blocking patterns. It is important for the tackle to think in terms of driving his shoulders through the gap to penetrate.

As the tackle penetrates, he needs to be able to defeat blockers at the point of attack if the ball is coming at him, or pursue the ball if it is moving laterally. The ability to use his hands is important for the tackle. He also needs to be able to use a forearm technique to defeat a blocker who is pulling to block him from the inside, such as the opposite-side guard or tackle. It is crucial that the tackle develop the ability to use these techniques to defeat blockers and pursue the football.

If the tackle is not blocked as he penetrates and the ball is moving laterally, he must be able to take as short or flat a course to the ball as possible. This ability to flatten his route is especially critical if the tackle is going to be a factor in plays run to the opposite side or in outside running plays on his side. In order to execute this skill effectively he must be able to come under control, with his weight distributed over his feet so he can change directions quickly. This type of reaction may be required on the first, second, or third steps, depending on how quickly the play develops. The tackle who can execute this technique effectively will be a productive player in this position. Although this skill is dependent on innate athletic ability, it can be developed and improved with practice. The drills to improve players in this area and others are covered in Chapter 9.

NOSE LINEBACKER

The nose linebacker in the Eagle defense is a unique position. This player needs to be part defensive lineman and part linebacker. He is asked to play over the center as a nose tackle lineman type of player and do all the things linemen do. However, he is also asked to drop off into pass coverage.

Physical and Mental Qualifications

Physically, the nose should be an inside linebacker type of player. That is, he does not have to be as big or physical a player as a defensive lineman. This position, because of the various responsibilities in the defenses, requires a player with linebacker instincts, movement, and quickness. Speed and quickness are more important than strength for the nose since he is a mover type rather than one who is asked to take on and defeat blockers on the line of scrimmage on a regular basis.

Football intelligence or the ability to put the game together mentally is very important to playing the nose linebacker position effectively. An awareness of offensive formation strengths and weaknesses as well as the necessary defensive adjustments to counter them is absolutely essential to playing this position well. Most linebackers in other defensive schemes acquire this type of information as part of their training and as a result, are well equipped to play the nose linebacker position.

Alignment

The nose linebacker lines up head on the offensive center. It is important that he vary his distance from on the line of scrimmage to as much as one yard off. This varying of the alignment on or off the line is important because it helps create uncertainty in the minds of the offensive blockers. The nose should move from one alignment to the other just before the snap. This movement is a very effective technique to create uncertainty in offensive players. The nose can also occasionally shade the center to the right or left. The side he shades depends on his responsibility on that specific play. For example, if his primary gap responsibility is to his right, he has the option to, just before the snap, stem a shade to his right. This would put him closer to his gap responsibility and make it more difficult for the center to block him on plays designed to go to his right.

Stance

The nose should use a balanced three-point stance. His weight should be distributed equally between the hand he has on the ground and his feet. His feet should be spread about shoulder width. This type of stance is necessary because he is asked to move laterally as well as forward and backward to execute his responsibilities.

Responsibilities

Run

The nose will get a call from the Mac linebacker on every down. The call will usually indicate to the nose that his gap responsibility will be the weakside "A" gap. Therefore, on the snap, he charges to his "A" gap responsibility. The nose may make a call to the tackle to the side of his

DIAGRAM 5–2
Nose Linebacker Right or Left Call

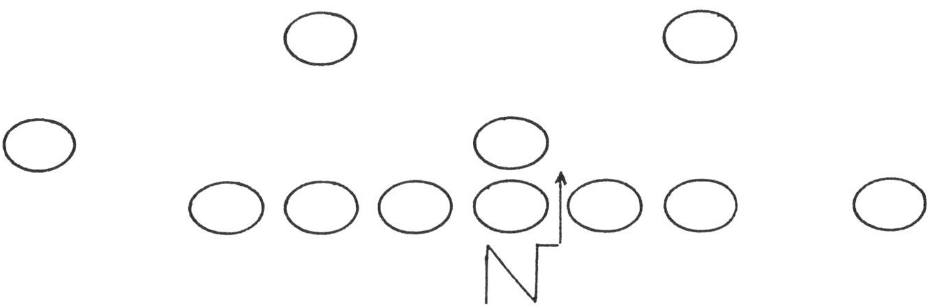

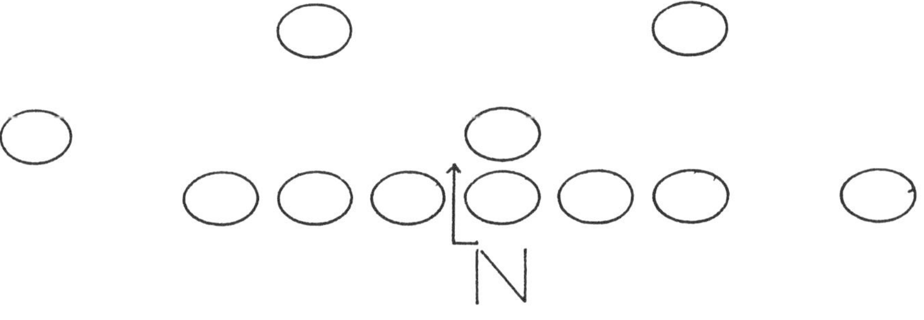

responsibility and run a game with him. When this call is made, the nose and tackle run the game and switch gap responsibility. The tackle has the "A" gap and the nose, the "B" gap.

Against some one-back formations, specifically those when Mac's man-for-man coverage lines up in the weak-back position, the nose may get a call to go to the strongside "A" gap. As a change-up, the nose can get a call to two-gap the center. With this call, the nose drives his hands into the center and is responsible for the "A" gap to the side of the play. (See Diagram 5–2.)

Pass

In any man-for-man coverage, dog, or blitz, the nose is a pass rusher on pass plays. He rushes through the "A" gap to the side of his respon-

DIAGRAM 5–3
Nose Linebacker Two-Gap Call

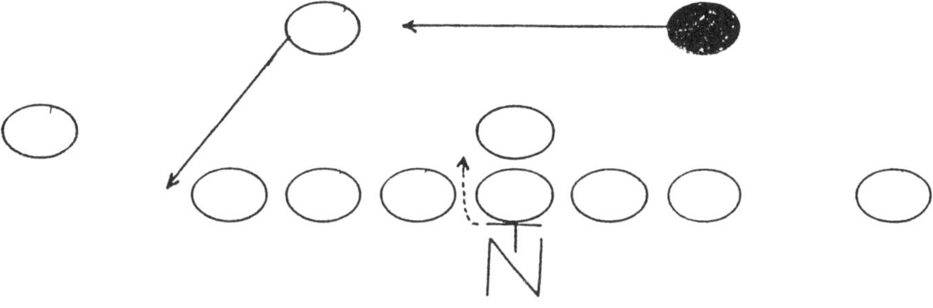

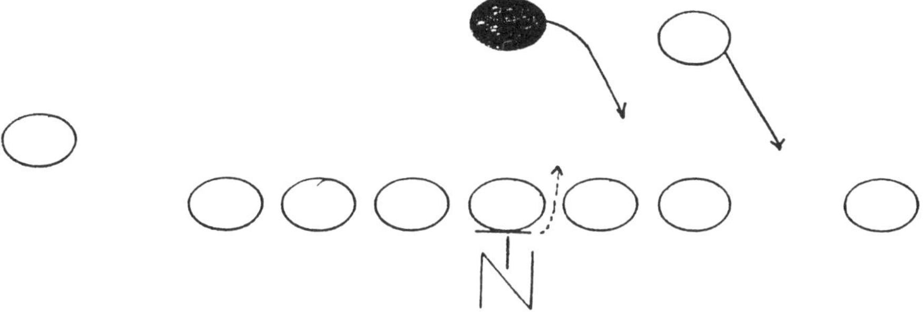

sibility. If a game is called between the tackle and nose, he rushes the passer through the "B" gap. If he has a two-gap call and a pass play develops, he should keep the quarterback in front of him and make a pass rush move off the corner or shoulder of the center to the side where the quarterback sets up. In most zone pass coverages, the nose is a hook defender to the weak side, or open side, of the formation. On the snap, he starts into the gap he is responsible for on running plays. As soon as he reads pass, he drops to his area of responsibility. (See Diagram 5–3.)

Techniques

The basic technique used by the nose is a slant, or angle, charge. This is the most important technique for the nose to perfect. He must develop the ability to move quickly laterally and penetrate at the same time. The technique is executed in two ways. One is a rip technique executed by the nose taking a parallel step with his right foot when he is going to his right. At the same time, he rips his left arm through the left shoulder of the center. He should be pushing with his right foot to penetrate. The slant-and-go is the other technique used by the nose. To execute this technique, the nose reaches for the center's shoulder pad on the side he is going to. For example, if he is going to the "A" gap to his right, he reaches with his hand to grab the left arm or shoulder of the center. As he reaches and grabs the center, he takes a short parallel step with his right foot. He pulls himself through the gap as he pushes with his right foot for penetration. He can either rip or use an arm-over or swim technique with his left arm as he splits the gap between the guard and center.

Games with Tackles

The nose can make a call to one of the tackles and exchange gap responsibilities. This is accomplished by executing one of the two types of games with the tackle. One is executed with the tackle charging into the "A" gap on the snap. At the same time, the nose comes around behind him and charges into the "B" gap. This allows time for the tackle to penetrate and disrupt the blocking schemes, as well as allows for the development of a shorter path to the ball for the nose. This game with the tackle going first is the one most frequently used. The other game is executed with the nose going first and charging into the "B" gap with the tackle charging behind the nose into the "A" gap. It is important that the lineman, who is the second man in these games, line up slightly deeper or off the line of scrimmage. This allows him to avoid being pinned on the line of scrimmage by an aggressive block and assures him space to operate and charge into the gap he is responsible for. It is, of course, important to vary these alignments on a consistent basis in order to disguise the games. If one or the other of these players lines up off the line of scrimmage only when they are executing a game, it serves to alert the offensive players and enhances their ability to block them. (See Diagram 5–4.)

Hands: Two-Gap

Although the nose linebacker is not asked to two-gap on a regular basis, he must learn to execute the technique. It is important in the teaching of the hands technique that the player learn to lead with the hands. All the movement of the hands and arms must be forward. There should be no winding up or hitching. The initial strength of the blow should come from the quickness with which the blow is struck. He must attack with his hands and then bring his feet with him. He cannot try to strike and step at the same time. If he does, his hands will be too slow. It is a

DIAGRAM 5–4
Nose Linebacker and Tackle Games

Right call with Tackle going first and Nose second.

Right call with Nose going first and Tackle second.

Left call with Tackle going first and Nose second.

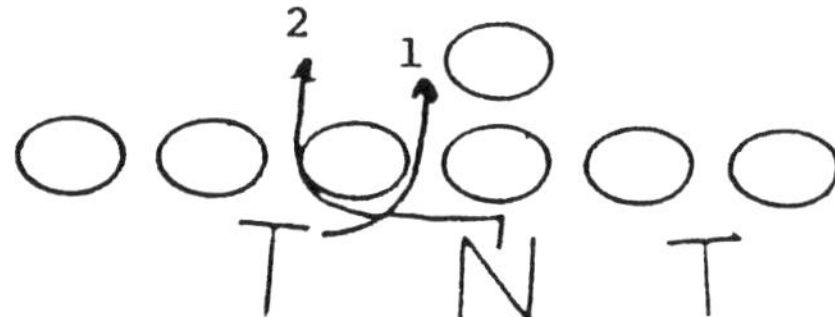

Left call with Nose going first and Tackle second.

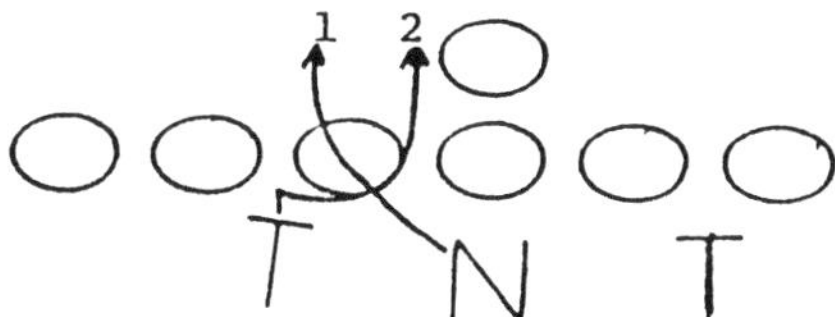

fact that the hands alone can get to the offensive player quicker if they are driven at the player without trying to step at the same time. The blow should be struck with the palms and heels of the hands. Where the blow is struck on the offensive blocker depends on the elevation of the blocker as he drives off the line of scrimmage. Ideally, any two-gap technique is executed best if the hands can be driven under the shoulder pads of the blocker or at the upper outside tips of the numbers on the front of the blocker's jersey. Again, however, the actual point of contact will be determined by the blocker's elevation. As the hands make contact with the blocker, the elbows should lock out, thereby involving the muscles of the back in the blow. Simultaneous with the lockout should be a rolling of the hips by flexing at the ankles, knees, and hips to involve the big muscles of the lower body. It is important that the feet be brought under the player in the two-gap technique. As the running play is read, the nose should shed or throw the blocker and accelerate upfield to the ball carrier.

Pass Rush

When the call dictates that the nose rush an "A" gap, he should make a pass rush move on the snap. His move should be made over the corner or shoulder of the center upfield for penetration. The counter to this move is to start the move to an "A" gap, and as the center overplays or moves into the gap, the nose should grab with the opposite hand and rush through the opposite "A" gap. When executing games with the tackle to rush the passer, if the nose is going first, he should penetrate at the snap into his gap. If he is the second man, he should allow the tackle to go first and collapse the area, creating a shorter route to the passer.

Pass Drop

In most zone defenses, the nose is a hook-to-curl defender on the weak side of the formation. His pre-snap right or left call should be to the side of his base run responsibility. Most of the time, this is consistent with the side of his hook-to-curl zone pass responsibility. If, by motion or shift, his pass responsibility should change, the nose merely adjusts after he reads pass and drops to the proper hook zone. He may also drop in pass coverage while using a two-gap technique on the center.

The technique is executed by the nose charging to his base run gap responsibility at the snap. He may be two-gapping the center, charging to an "A" gap, or executing a game with a tackler. As soon as he reads a pass play, he drops to his pass zone. It is important that he look back at the line of scrimmage as he drops so he can see the release of the number-two receiver on his side of the formation (usually the halfback).

The release of the number-two receiver tells him how much width he must get in his initial drop. It is also important for him to be looking back to see the quarterback for any quick throw or three-step drop action. If the nose is facing the line of scrimmage as he drops, he is in a position to see and react to any draw plays or other pass-related plays. This position also allows him to see the quarterback and react to where he looks and throws the ball. (See Diagram 5–5.)

DIAGRAM 5–5
Nose Linebacker Zone Drops from Line Charge Variations

Right call - weak hook drop.

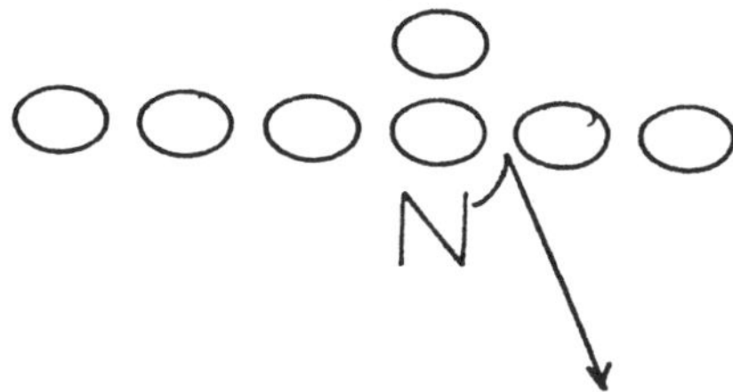

Left call - weak hook drop.

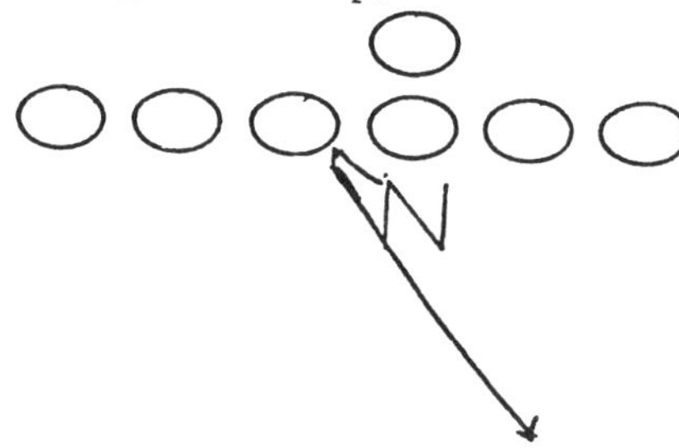

Two-gap call - weak hook drop.

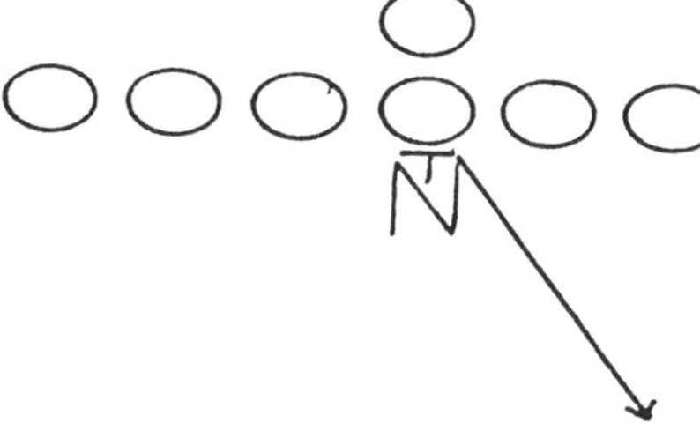

Right call with game - tackle first - nose starts to run gap responsibility - when he reads pass, takes his weak hook drop.

THE "B" BACKER
(Linebacker Who Lines Up Over the Tight End)

The "B" linebacker position is one of the most demanding in the defense. He must be able to defeat the tight end's base block as well as cover him man-to-man all over the field. In addition, he must be a competent zone defender. The best type of player to use in this position is one who is trained as an outside linebacker in a 34 or 4–3 scheme.

Physical Qualifications

Strength is important, especially if the "B" backer is going to be successful in defeating the tight end. Strength in the hands and arms, or upper body strength, is the most beneficial. Next in importance is speed as it relates to pass coverage ability. It is reasonable to expect that if he is asked to cover tight ends man-for-man, he should be able to run as fast as they can. Quickness is important as it relates to pass coverage and the ability to accelerate off blocks and make tackles. The ability to use his hands is the single most important physical quality he can possess when it comes to defeating the blocks of the tight end. This allows him to use his strength, gain operating space or separation from the blocker, and shed the blocker. The ability to change directions quickly enables the "B" linebackers to adjust their angles to the ball against runs and to execute their responsibilities effectively in man or zone coverages. This position is more a mechanical position than an instinctive one. In other words, a player can be taught and drilled on all the necessary responses and play the position well even though he may not be a gifted instinctive player.

Alignment

His alignment is on the line of scrimmage and may vary from head up to a slight inside or outside shade on the tight end. Although he may vary his alignment, he must not compromise his ability to play his base gap responsibility. The factors that affect the alignment of the "B" backer are the splits of the tight end. If the tight end lines up tight to his tackle, the backer will line up head up to a slight outside shade. If he flexes, the alignment will be head up to inside shade. If the linebacker can dominate the tight end physically he will be more inclined to line up head up on him. The coverage calls will also affect how he lines up. In zone coverages when he is a hook defender, he will line up head up to inside shade on the tight end. When he is a flat defender, he will line up head up to slight outside shade. In man coverages when he is covering the tight end man-for-man, he will line up inside shade. However, when he is playing in and out with the Mac on the tight end and strong back, he will line up outside shade on the tight end.

Stance

The stance is the up position usually assumed by a linebacker. It should be a slightly staggered stance with the inside foot up. There should be good flexion, or bend, at the ankles, knees, and hips. He should have good body lean, with the weight distributed over the balls of the feet. The hands and arms should be relaxed but ready to use.

Responsibility

Run

In nearly all coverages and variations, the base run-gap responsibility is the "C" gap for the "B" backer. However, when he is involved in an in-and-out call with Mac and he assumes an outside alignment, his base gap responsibility is the "D" gap, squeezing the "C" gap with the blocker on runs to his side. On runs designed to go to the other side of the formation, he should pursue flat down the line of scrimmage and take the most direct course to the ball.

Pass

Probably the most difficult assignment the "B" backer has in defending the pass is to cover the tight end man-for-man. This is his pass responsibility more often than any other in man coverages, dogs, and blitzes. He will also play in-and-out coverage with the Mac linebacker on the tight end and near back. In zone coverages, he is a curl-to-flat defender if the secondary is rotating away from him. If the secondary is rotating to his side, the "B" backer is a hook-to-curl defender. In two-deep zone coverages, it is his responsibility to cover the tight end man-for-man on all routes except quick flat or shallow crossing routes.

Techniques

Run

The hands, or two-gap, technique is the most crucial skill the "B" backer must develop. It is basically the same technique used by the defensive lineman. The only difference is that the linemen execute it from a down position, while the "B" backer plays from an up stance. On the snap, the hands are driven for the outside upper tips of the tight end's numbers. The blow is struck with the palms and heels of the hands working for extension and a locking out at the elbows. At the same time, the hips should be rolled in to involve the big muscles. In order to ensure a leverage advantage over the blocker, he should have good flexion at the ankles, knees, and hips. His power position will be enhanced by having his shoulder level lower than that of the blocker. The objective is to knock the tight end back and create a new line of scrimmage. This working upfield of the tight end is important in defending off-tackle and outside running plays. He cannot be washed down or blocked down the line of scrimmage. It is permissible for him to play upfield under hook or reach blocks by the tight end. It is important that the "B" backers see the near back's action and the pulling lane, which is the area that is about two yards behind the line of scrimmage and extends from one offensive tackle position to the other. The "B" linebacker should meet and defeat all blockers coming from the inside out on the offensive side of the line of scrimmage, about $1\frac{1}{2}$ yards deep. He must hold his outside position and close the inside holes with the blocker's body. His rule is to defeat all blockers from the inside with his hands or inside shoulder and forearm. While he is defeating blockers he should strive to keep his hips and shoulders as parallel as possible to the line of scrimmage.

Pass

The most important factor in man-for-man coverage for the "B" backer is to maintain an inside position. Therefore, to start from an inside alignment is definitely beneficial. The proper technique involves the driving of the outside hand at the outside upper tips of the tight end's numbers at the snap. It is important that the inside foot remain stationary and that he pivot off it and open his hips by picking up his outside foot. As the tight end releases outside, the "B" backer should jam him with his inside hand into the shoulder or armpit, flattening his route on the release. It is important that through this process of jam and release, the "B" backer not cross his feet over. As the tight end releases outside, he should establish a man-for-man trail technique. That is, a position one yard inside and one yard behind the tight end. During the pass route, there should be complete concentration on the pocket or the hands of the receiver.

If the "B" backer is involved with in-and-out coverage on the tight end and near back with Mac, his coverage responsibility on an inside release by the tight end will be the back. With in-and-out coverage, his alignment should be head up to outside shade on the tight end. If the tight end releases inside, he should come across the line using an aggressive catch technique on the back. It is important that he establish an inside position with his inside leg and jam, just as he would on a tight end. If the back tries to release inside, he should jam him into the line of scrimmage. On an outside release jam, he must keep his feet moving through the jam, establish and hold his inside position, and concentrate on the hands or the pocket the receiver makes with his hands to catch the ball. It is important that the "B" backer not look back for the ball. He must make his plays on the ball by driving his hands and arms through the pocket as the receiver attempts to catch it.

In zone coverages, he is a curl-to-flat defender most of the time. In order to best allow him to execute his responsibility, he should use a head up to outside shade alignment. On the snap, as he reads pass, he should start a 45-degree angle drop aiming for a position 12 to 14 yards deep inside the wide receiver. As he drops, he must get his eyes back on the quarterback in order to read a quick, or three-step, drop. If there is no three-step drop, he continues his drop holding off the curl to either force it inside to the hook defender or give the hook defender time to widen to it. The "B" backer will stretch or widen with any quick throw. It is important that he have his weight distributed over the balls of his feet during the drop. This allows him to be under control and react to a throw by the passer at any time during his drop. It is also crucial that he be taught to drive on all balls thrown in front of him at the proper angle. Generally, it is crucial that he drive to put the ball on his inside pad on all balls thrown in his area. This allows him to always drive with great velocity, knowing he has other players driving from the inside. If he should miss a tackle, other players will be in position to make it. On quick screens, he should drive inside out, making the tackle with his outside shoulder pad. The corner is the outside defender on quick screens. On slow screens, the "B" backer is the outside man and should drive to put the ball on his inside pad.

If the rotation of the secondary is to the "B" backer, he is a hook-to-curl defender. With hook responsibility, his alignment should be head up to inside shade on the tight end. On the snap, he must jam and wall the tight end or force him up the field and not let him inside quick. Since the tight end is the number-two receiver to his side, his release determines how much width or stretch the "B" backer needs to get in his drop. He must see the quarterback for three-step drop and react to the quarterback's look and throw. Generally, the hook zone extends laterally from the middle of the offensive formation to the curl area and vertically about 12 to 14 yards from the line of scrimmage. His pattern reads are the number-two and number-three receivers to his side of the formation. They determine the amount of lateral stretch, expand, or collapse he can get as he executes his responsibility. Body position is important, especially low shoulder level. If he does not raise up at the snap he will be able to play with his feet under him and be in the best possible position to react to patterns and the look and throw of the quarterback. On all throws in front of the hook defenders, it is important that he drive with great velocity. He can do this best by being aware of where his help is. As a hook defender, the "B" backer should drive to put all throws inside him on his inside shoulder pad and all outside throws on his outside pad. This allows him to drive with great velocity, knowing that if he misses, the next adjacent player in the rotation will be there to make the tackle. On all screens, the "B" backer should drive with an inside-out angle, making the tackle with his outside shoulder pad.

6

The Second Level

This chapter discusses the second-level positions in the Eagle defense—the Mac linebacker and the strong safety—in detail. It describes the physical and mental requirements for these positions, as well as the alignment, stance, and responsibilities of each. Diagram 6–1 illustrates the alignment of the second level in the Eagle defense.

MAC LINEBACKER

To play this position well a player must not only be a gifted player physically, he must also be well equipped from a mental standpoint. The Mac must make the defensive calls in the huddle and make the audible calls for adjustments. In short, he is the coach on the field.

Physical and Mental Qualifications

Football instincts rate high as a quality he must be well endowed with. Quickness is an essential quality, as it will allow him to get to his responsibilities on run and pass more efficiently. Speed is as important as any characteristic, especially since he is required to cover the tight end or backs man-for-man as well as make plays on the run from sideline to sideline. Although the Mac is well protected and does not have to take on blockers nearly as frequently as he does in other schemes, strength, especially in the upper body, does help him execute better at the point of attack. The ability to change directions quickly enables the Mac to take the shortest, most direct path, or course, to the ball on running plays as well as to make plays in the passing game. Again, although blockers do not get

43

DIAGRAM 6–1
Eagle Defense: An Eight-Man Front

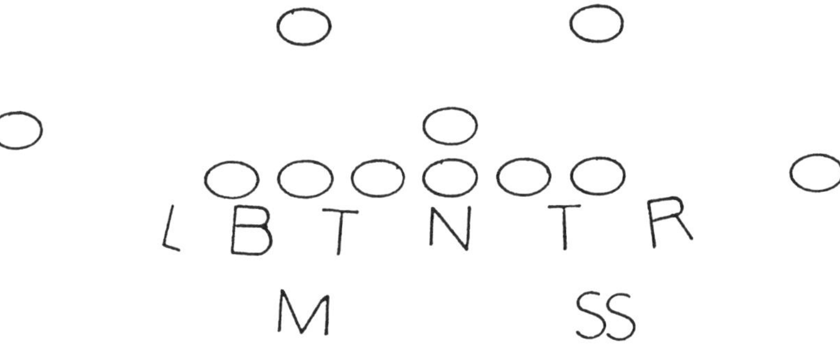

Any alignment or adjustment that puts the strong safety within
five yards of the line of scrimmage lined up inside the L or
R creates an eight-man front.

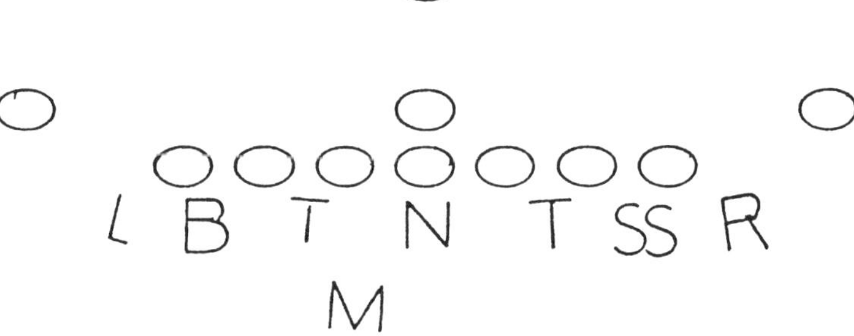

Whenever adjustments in the Eagle Defense cause the strong
safety to align outside the L or R, the offense is forced
out of the eight-man front.

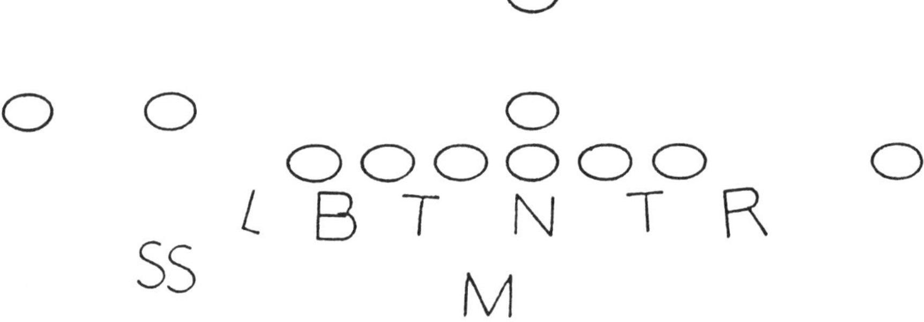

many clear shots at the Mac, he does have to have the ability to avoid defeat and accelerate off blockers! This requires the ability to use his hands, shed and throw a blocker, and accelerate to the ball carrier. Equally important is the ability to finesse, or dodge, the blockers.

Mentally he must have the ability to understand the game from a technical standpoint. There are many mechanical positions in football where a player can learn to play them well without much in the way of instincts. The Mac linebacker position is not one of them. He must have the ability to learn and understand offenses and defenses. He must have a willingness to study and prepare more than any other defensive team member. He must be willing to spend inordinate amounts of time with film study and meetings. The ability to lead is important for the Mac—to lead by his example and to demand that other team members perform at a high level are essential qualities.

Alignment

The Mac lines up 4 to 4½ yards off the line of scrimmage. Against two-back formations his general alignment laterally is in the area of the offensive tackle on the strong side, or tight-end side, of the formation. As a general rule, if there is a back lined up in the halfback position on the tight-end side of the formation, he lines up on him. If there is no back lined up in this position, he can cheat his alignment to a stacked position directly behind the defensive tackle. He may line up stacked over the inside leg of his tackle if there is a strong weakside run tendency from this type of formation. Against one-back formations, with the back behind the center, he will line up opposite the gap between the guard and center on the strong side. If the back lines up in the halfback position strongside, he should line up opposite him. If the back lines up in the halfback position weakside, he should line up opposite the "A" gap weakside. If the Mac lines up in the weak "A" gap because of the back's alignment, he should send the nose to the strongside "A" gap with his call. The adjustments in the Mac alignment are necessary to put him in the best possible position to play his base run-gap responsibility. It is even more important to pass defense because in man-for-man coverages he must be in the best possible position to cover the back.

Stance

The best stance for the Mac to use is the up position with a slight toe and heel stagger. He should have good flexion at the ankles, knees, and hips, and he should have his weight distributed over the balls of his feet. He should feel comfortable in his stance and have the ability to go right or left—forward or backward—with the same ease of movement.

Keep and Responsibility

Keys

The Mac keys the near back, or the back closest to him in the backfield set, and the ball through the offensive linemen. Although he is focused on the back and the ball handling, he must be able to see the type of blocking being used by the offensive linemen. The ability to read the blocking scheme enables the Mac to determine quickly the specific part of the defense the running play is designed to attack.

Responsibilities

Run

There are two basic types of running plays that can be run to a side of the defense. One is a direct-read play, which is a run designed to attack the "A" or "B" gaps. In this type of play the blockers and the ball carrier are attacking the line of scrimmage straight ahead. Dives, traps, leads, and whams are examples of these types of plays. On direct-read plays the Mac must take blockers on with his hands or inside arm control, close the inside with the blocker, and make these plays from the outside in.

It is important that the Mac sprint toward the line of scrimmage to meet and defeat the blockers on these types of plays. He cannot stop to take the blockers on. The quicker he can get to the holes and close the holes, the more effective he will be.

The other type of running play is a fast read. These are running plays that are designed to attack off-tackle in the "C" gap or outside in the "D" gap. When the Mac reads these types of plays, he must establish a downhill or attack angle toward the line of scrimmage. As he works downhill he is establishing an inside-out angle to the ball. He should make all plays from the inside out with a good up-and-in angle attacking the line of scrimmage. The inside-out and up-and-in angle allows him to take the inside cutback away from the ball carrier. Whenever possible, the defensive player must take something away from the ball carrier by his angle to the ball. This helps him avoid the problem of being one-on-one or head up on a great back. When these situations arise, the ball carrier has a tremendous advantage due to the athletic skill differential. I believe it is the coaches' responsibility to avoid putting defensive players in these positions by teaching players the proper way to reduce angles and take away options for the ball carrier. It is important that the play of the "B" backer and the Mac against fast-read runs be coordinated. If the "B" backer is lined up inside, he is responsible for the "C" gap, which means the Mac must scrape up and in to the "D" gap. Conversely, if the "B" backer is lined up outside shade on the tight end, he is responsible for the "D" gap, and the Mac must take the "C" gap on all outside runs to the strong side of the formations.

On runs to the opposite side of the formation the Mac is responsible for the backside "A" gap—that is, the "A" gap to Mac's side of the center. Since the nose will be committed to the weakside "A" gap most of the time, Mac will be responsible for the strongside "A" gap on weakside plays. However, if the nose is committed to the strongside "A" gap by call, then Mac would have the "A" gap weakside on this type of run. It is important to note here that Mac attacks the "A" gap backside in proportion to how much the ball is attacking at a straight-ahead or downhill angle. The more the ball is being handed off downhill or toward the line of scrimmage, the more the Mac must attack his "A" gap. These are direct-read plays to the opposite side of the formation. On fast-read plays to the opposite side, he can move in more of a lateral fashion since the chances of cutback are reduced by the design of the play. As the Mac attacks the weakside "A" gap, it is important that he either use his hands and two-gap the blocker or use his strongside arm to control the blocker. If he tries to defeat the blocker with his weakside arm, he will be cut off from his gap responsibility.

Pass

In man-for-man coverages the Mac is responsible for the fullback or strong back in two-back formations. He will usually be involved with the "B" backer in combination coverage on the fullback and tight end. This in-and-out coverage is based on the release of the tight end and the flow or release of the two backs. If the tight end releases inside and the strong back releases to the strong side, the Mac covers the tight end, and the "B" backer covers the back. If the tight end releases outside, the "B" backer covers him, and the Mac covers the back if he releases strongside. If the strong back blocks or releases to the weak side, the Mac and strong safety play in-and-out coverage on the two backs. When both backs go weak and weak flow occurs, the "B" backer covers the tight end on all releases. Versus one-back formations, the Mac covers the remaining back man-for-man.

He is a strongside hook-to-curl defender in most zone coverage situations. However, there are times when he is required to be a weakside hook-to-curl defender. This change of sides occurs against trips formations when a three-deep zone defense has been called. He must play all screens inside out in zone coverages.

See Diagrams 6–2 and 6–3 for descriptions and illustrations of the in-and-out reads.

DIAGRAM 6–2
Eagle Mac and "B" Backer In-and-Out Reads

Tight end inside release and FB release or block strong side Mac
has tight end man-for-man and "B" has FB man-for-man.

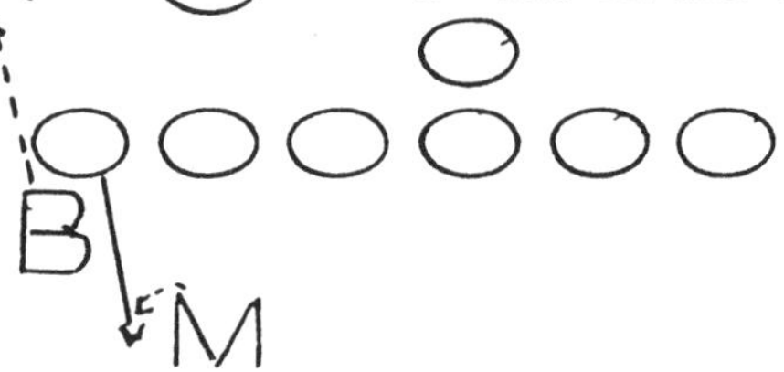

Tight end outside release and FB release strongside or weakside
"B" backer has tight end man-for-man and Mac has FB man-for-man.

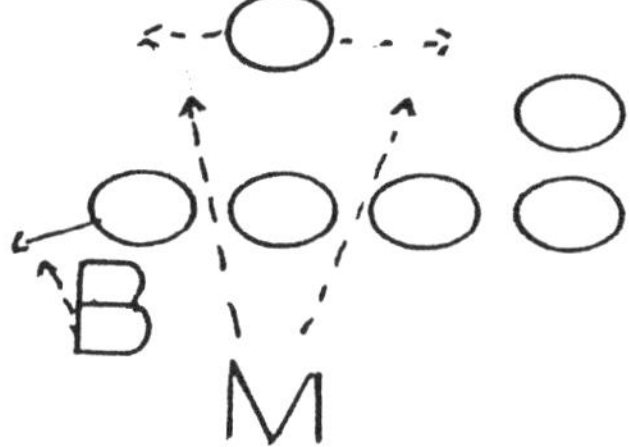

Tight end inside release inside and FB release or block weakside
"B" has tight end man-for-man and Mac has FB man-for-man.

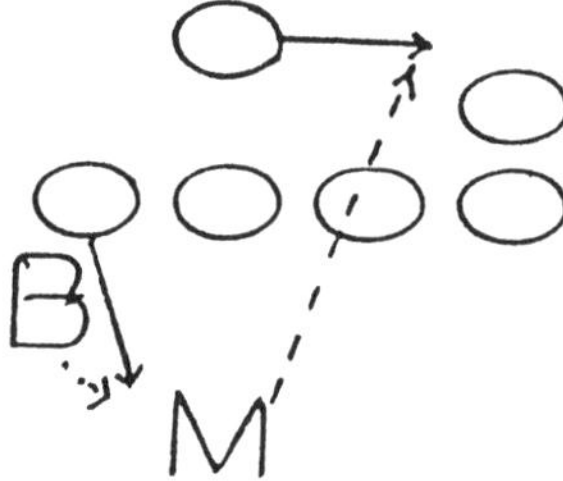

Tight end pass blocks "B" backer has tight end and Mac has FB
man-for-man.

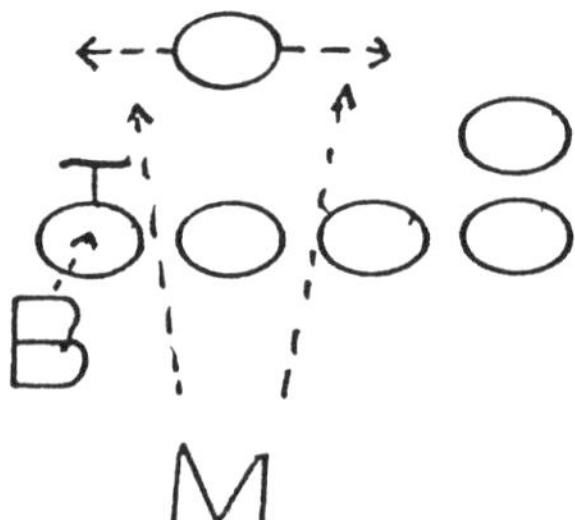

DIAGRAM 6–3
Eagle Mac and Strong Safety In-and-Out Reads

Both backs release strongside-Mac has first back (FB) man-for-man
and strong safety has second back (HB) man-for-man.

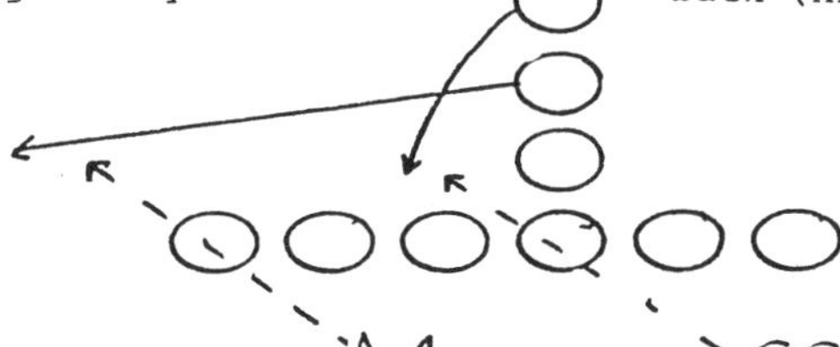

Both backs release weakside-strong safety has first back (FB) man-for-
man and Mac has second back (HB) man-for-man.

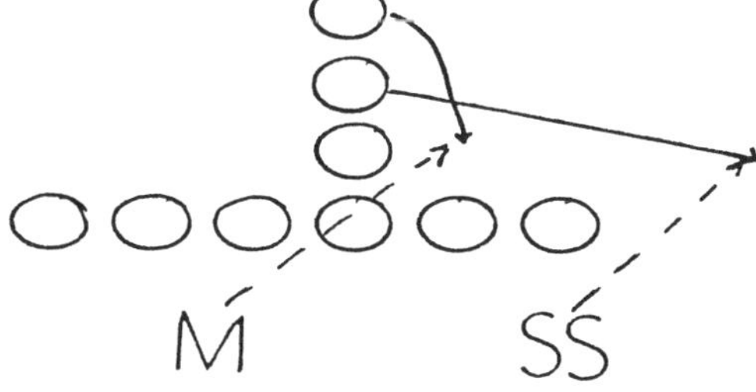

Both backs strongside pick release – Mac has widest back strongside
(HB) man-for-man and strong safety has nearest back to him (FB) man-
for-man.

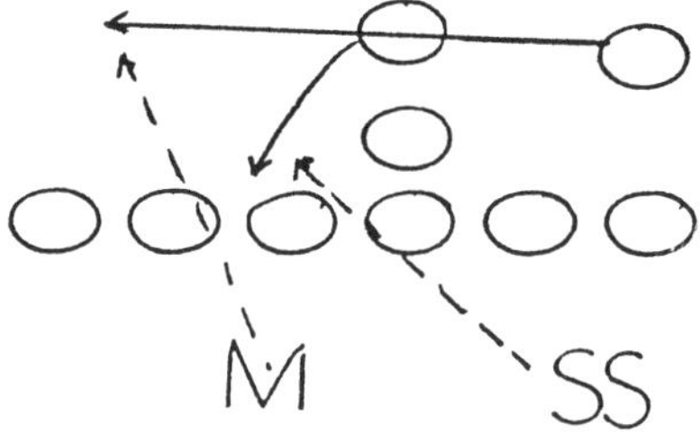

Both backs weakside pick release – strong safety has widest back (FB)
man-for-man and Mac has nearest back (HB) man-for-man.

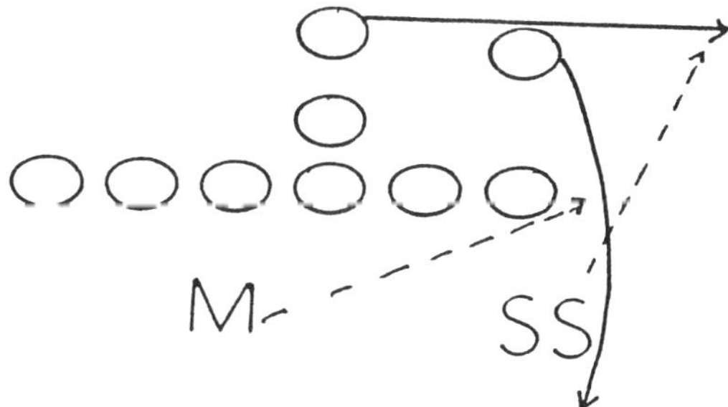

Techniques

Hands

In any defense, inside linebackers must be able to use their hands to defeat and ward off blockers. Even though the Mac linebacker in the Eagle defense is protected and does not have any offensive linemen who have a clean release to block him, he must learn to use his hands. On running plays the hands technique must be accompanied by the ability to use his feet to accelerate off blocks. The technique is executed by striking with the palms and heels of the hands at the outside tips of the front numbers or under the shoulder pads of the offensive blocker. As contact is made, the elbows lock to involve the back muscles and at the same time the hips are rolled to involve the big muscles. Leverage comes from keeping the shoulder level lower than that of the blocker and involves good flexion, or bend, at the ankles, knees, and hips by the Mac. It is important that the hands technique be taught as a skill the Mac executes on the move. He cannot stop to hit or take on blockers. He has to learn to be in perpetual motion exploding into blockers and accelerating off them. If he has to stop to hit, he is not able to accelerate effectively off blocks and make plays on the ball carriers.

The Mac must also learn to finesse blockers with his hands and feet. This is accomplished by driving the hands at the blocker and just before contact is made, pulling the hands back and slipping around or under the blocker to the ball carrier. This technique is especially beneficial when a blocker has great momentum as he approaches the Mac. All technique versus the run must be executed on the move at good angles toward the line of scrimmage, the blocker, and the ball carriers. On direct reads or inside runs, the angle the Mac takes to the ball should be straight ahead but with the objective to make the tackle with his inside shoulder pad or from the outside in. On fast reads or outside plays, his angle should be up and in or toward the line of scrimmage with an inside-out angle on the blockers and ball carriers.

Pass

The man-for-man coverage technique used by the Mac is what I call an inside-out catch technique. It is important that he establish an inside position on the receiver and not lose it. If his coverage is the tight end, as soon as he reads pass and an inside release he must step up to ensure that he prevents a quick flat release. He wants to force the tight end upfield with his inside position. If the tight end persists in trying to release in front of the Mac, he should physically jam him into the line of scrimmage. If his coverage is a back, he should step up as soon as he reads pass to establish an inside position. The Mac should move toward the back from the inside out striving to junction or jam him. By using his hands on the back, the Mac is attempting to force him to release upfield and outside. If the back tries to release inside or across the formation, the Mac should jam him into the line of scrimmage. In all man coverages the Mac should establish a position on the receiver about one yard inside and one yard behind him as he runs his pass route. The Mac should concentrate on the receiver's hands or "the pocket" and physically drive through the hands to strip the ball as it is caught. Again, the Mac should never look back at the quarterback once he is committed to coverage upfield on a receiver. If the Mac looks back, it will allow the receiver to adjust his route and make it impossible for him to defend the pass.

Zone

The proper execution of zone coverage technique requires the Mac to play with good body position. It starts with a good stance and requires that he not raise up out of his stance as he drops to his area of responsibility. If he does not raise up, but keeps his shoulder level constant, he ensures that his weight is distributed over the balls of his feet. This places him in a position to be able to react and change directions at any time during his pass drop. When the Mac reads pass and starts his drop to his outside at about a 45-degree angle, he must see the release of the number-two receiver to his side. The release by the Y on the strong side determines how much width he needs to get in his initial drop. As he opens his hips he must keep his shoulders as parallel as he can with the line of scrimmage. This ensures that he will be in a position to see the quarterback, where he is looking and when he is throwing the ball. He should be working to a depth of 10 to 12 yards. If the quarterback throws the ball anytime during the drop, the Mac must take the proper angle and drive on the throw. It is important that as a hook or underneath defender the Mac be coached to drive or break on the ball as soon as the quarterback turns his shoulders and looks to throw. If he does not break on the look, he will have difficulty making plays. It is also important that a hook defender drive with great velocity on any ball thrown in front of him. If a ball is thrown inside, he must drive to make the tackle with his inside shoulder. If it is thrown outside, he must drive to make the tackle with his outside shoulder. This ensures that he will be driving to make a tackle and at the same time forcing the receiver into an area where another defender will be driving to make a tackle from the opposite side. The simple rule for any underneath inside defender is that if the ball is caught inside, you drive to make the tackle with your inside shoulder pad—if it is caught outside, drive to make the tackle with your outside pad. This approach ensures that the Mac can drive with great velocity on short throws, knowing that if he misses the tackle a teammate will be coming from the other side to make it. If the quarterback is holding the ball and not giving an indication of the direction he is throwing, the Mac must continue to get depth. Again, it is important that he not raise his shoulder level since this slows his ability to react. Not raising his shoulder level and being able to see the quarterback are the two most important factors in zone technique for the Mac.

The alignment of the number-two receiver in the formation affects the Mac's drop in some situations. For example, in a trips formation with the number-two receiver lined up wide, the Mac must start with a wider angle to his drop. However, when he is lined up to the tight-end side of a slot formation, his initial drop will be straight back. There should be no opening of the hips; his backpedal should be straight back.

STRONG SAFETY

The ideal player for this position should have the physical qualities of a linebacker and the coverage ability of a defensive back. He should be the most physical of the defensive backs on the team.

Physical and Mental Qualifications

Strength is important to the strong safety in that it enables him to execute his run responsibilities. He has the same blocking threats as both the Mac and "B" linebackers. When he is lined up as a linebacker on the weak side he can be blocked by a guard, tackle, or back. In some two-tight-end formation adjustments he must play over and defeat a tight end. Therefore, explosive strength is an essential physical quality the strong safety must possess. Speed is important because it allows the strong safety to chase down running plays to his side as well as those that go away from him. It is especially important, when the R or L bounces a play outside, that the strong safety have the speed and athletic ability to chase it down and make the tackle. The faster the strong safety can run, the better chance he has to cover his responsibility in man coverages. Quickness enables him to adjust his paths to the ball in the running game, finesse blockers, and cover quick receivers. The ability to change directions well really enables him to react to plays that start inside but actually end up outside. It also helps him to play better in space or when adjustments cause him to play outside against one-back formations. Since this is essentially a linebacker position and things happen so quickly, all the physical and mental qualities required to play Mac well are critical. Instincts, the ability to defeat and avoid blockers, as well as the ability to accelerate off blocks, are all essential. The ability to tackle well certainly is high on the list of very important qualifications for playing the position well.

Alignment

Against two-back formations, the strong safety should line up from three to seven yards off the line of scrimmage head up to outside shoulder on the open side, or weakside, offensive tackle. He should line up closer to the line of scrimmage and wider against offensive formations that are basic weakside running sets. For example, versus an opposite set or a formation with a fullback behind the center and a halfback setting in the weak-back position, he should line up three yards off the line of scrimmage on the outside shoulder of the tackle. Versus any two tight-end formations, with the second tight end lined up to weakside on the line of scrimmage, he should line up on him on the line of scrimmage head up to inside shade. Against balanced one-back formations, he should line up over the number-two receiver weakside three to seven yards off the line of scrimmage. His alignment against a trips formation should be over the number-two receiver strongside three to seven yards off the line of scrimmage.

Stance

The stance used by the strong safety should be similar to the one used by the Mac linebacker. He plays from the up position with his weight distributed over the balls of his feet. He should have good flexion at the ankles, knees, and hips and should have a slight toe and heel stagger. As he moves deeper or wider in his alignment, he will play from a higher stance or one more characteristically used by a defensive back. The lower linebacker type of stance is necessary when the strong safety is playing in a confined area. When he is playing over a tight end, he uses his linebacker stance. In this situation he must be ready to defeat the block of the tight end.

Keep and Responsibility

Key

The strong safety keys the near back but also must see the blocking-pattern scheme of the offensive play. As he focuses on the back and the ball handling he should be able to see the action of the offensive linemen. When he is lined up over a tight end, he keys through the tight end to the near back and the pulling lane.

Responsibilities

Run

Running plays that are designed to attack the "A" and "B" gaps weakside are direct-read plays. On these types of actions the strong safety must attack the line of scrimmage just as the Mac linebacker does on the strong side. He must make these plays from the outside in putting blockers and the ball carrier on his inside shoulder pad. On fast-read or wide plays, he must take a good downhill up-and-in angle and work inside out to the ball. He must always be in a position to chase down any runs that the R or L linebackers have forced to bounce outside. On most runs to the strong side of the formation, he has the strongside "A" gap. However, if the nose linebacker is committed to the strongside "A" gap by the call, the strong safety is responsible for the weakside "A" gap. Against some one-back formations, in zone coverages, the strong safety becomes the force man. He is responsible for forcing the run whenever his alignment is outside the R or L. This occurs versus wide trips or wide double formations. This call allows the R or L to play hard inside with no run force responsibility due to the fact that the strong safety is a force man outside him.

Pass

In man-for-man coverages the strong safety is responsible for the number-two receiver weakside in all formations except trips and two-back sets. In a trips formation his pass coverage responsibility is the number-two receiver to the strong side. In a slot formation he is responsible for the number-three receiver to the strong side. Versus two-back formations, he and the Mac linebacker will play in-and-out coverage on the H and F on any action where both backs release to the strong or weak side of the formation. The zone coverage responsibility of the strong safety is the weakside curl-to-flat zone. However, against a trips formation he becomes a curl-to-flat defender on the strong side. In two-deep zone coverages he is a deep half defender. That is why it is important for the strong safety to stem or change his alignment. This prevents him from giving away the coverage by lining up in a deep alignment only when he is a two-deep safety.

Technique

The techniques used by the strong safety are similar to those used by the Mac linebacker. He must be able to use his hands to defeat and accelerate off blocks. He must also be able to avoid and finesse blockers. When he is lined up over a tight end, he must be able to use his hands and defeat his block. In short, he must develop the same run defense skills as the Mac and "B" backer. However, because he is not as big a player physically as they are, he must use finesse techniques more.

On all inside runs he will use the hands or a forearm technique to defeat blockers. As he takes on blockers he must be sprinting to the line of scrimmage, strike under the shoulder pads of the blocker with his hands, making plays from the outside in. If he is using a forearm technique, he should strike with the inside arm, keeping his outside arm and leg free as he squeezes the hole. He will also use the drop-step technique where he fakes taking on the blocker, avoids them, and makes the tackle.

There are three basic techniques the strong safety uses in executing his responsibilities against outside runs. Two of the three are finesse techniques. The slip technique is executed by the strong safety driving under the blocker with an inside-out angle to the ball carrier. He may also execute the technique by faking an angle across the blocker, getting the blocker to overcommit upfield, then coming under him to tackle the ball carrier. The slide technique is executed by playing over the blocker to the ball carrier. It may also be executed by the strong safety faking as though he were going under the blocker or using a slip technique, then coming across the face of the blocker to the ball carrier. The third technique is the leverage technique, which involves the strong safety driving through the blocker to the ball carrier. It may also be executed by the strong safety knocking the blocker into the ball carrier. It is very important that the strong safety spend time in individual period with the Mac linebackers and the "B" linebackers. This gives him the opportunity to acquire and develop the skills essential for playing the position well.

Pass

In man-for-man coverage the strong safety is responsible for covering the weak back or the H in a normal two-back formation. He uses the same inside-out catch techniques that the Mac linebacker uses. As soon as he reads pass, the strong safety should move toward the line of scrimmage to establish an inside position on the receiver. He should work to junction or jam the back with his hands and take away the option of the back making an inside pass cut. He uses a trail technique on all upfield routes, striving to keep a yard behind and a yard inside the receiver. He must keep his concentration on the hands or the pocket as he covers the back up the field. When he jams or junctions the receivers, he strives to change his route. If the receiver tries to release inside or under the strong safety, he must jam him into the line of scrimmage. When he is covering a number-two receiver in balanced one-back or trips formations, he uses an inside man-for-man technique. This means he must challenge the receiver on all routes and never permit him to beat him quick inside. He will either execute his responsibility against one-back formations from the off position seven yards off the line of scrimmage or from the up or press position on the line of scrimmage.

Zone

The strong safety in zone coverages will be a curl-to-flat defender on most zone coverages. His angle of drop must be to a point where he is driving to the curl area. The aiming point is about two yards inside the number, 10 to 12 yards deep. When he is lined up opposite the offensive tackle, as he is against two-back formations, he will open at a flatter angle than when he is lined up outside, as he is in one-back formations. After he reads pass and begins his drop to his curl-to-flat responsibility, he must get his head back on the quarterback in order to read whether or not he is throwing a pass from a three-step drop. If there is no three-step drop but the quarterback is working weakside, he must hold off the curl and be ready to drive on any outside throw to the number-two receiver weak. It is important that he hold off the curl until the hook defender has time to stretch to it. As a curl-to-flat defender he must drive to put all receivers who catch balls in front of him on his inside shoulder pad as he tackles them. It is important that he do this in order to ensure that he can drive on all cuts with velocity; should he miss, he will be driving the receiver back into the other defenders. The alignment or split of the wide receivers and the alignment of the strong safety are the initial factors that determine the strong safety's angle of drop. The specific patterns run by the number-one and number-two receivers to the weak side are the other factors that determine how the zone pass drop techniques of the strong safety are executed. He should make all plays on slow screens from the outside in and quick screens from the inside.

In two-deep zone coverage the strong safety is responsible for the weakside deep half of the field. It is important that he stem his alignment to a depth of about 7 to 10 yards from the line of scrimmage. As the ball is snapped he must get depth and work for a point two yards inside the numbers. As he gets depth he must read the routes of the number-one and number-two receivers weakside. If both the number-two and number-one receivers are working up the field, he must continue to drop and place himself in a position to make a play on a ball thrown to either receiver. If only one of the weakside receivers releases up the field, he must continue to get depth, working for a position to be able to make a play on any ball thrown upfield to him.

7

The Three Deep

This chapter discusses the three deep defenders of the Eagle defense—the free safety and two corners—in detail. It describes the physical and mental requirements for these positions, as well as the alignment, stance, and responsibilities of each. Diagram 7–1 shows these positions in a normal Eagle alignment and in two variations.

FREE SAFETY

The free safety has to have the pass coverage ability of a cornerback. Many of the adjustments in the Eagle defense require him to cover a wide receiver in situations when the offense uses three wide receivers. A good run player who is a good tackler is a real asset in this position. Since the free safety is unaccounted for in most blocking schemes, he has many opportunities to make tackles on running plays. However, the ability to play pass defense is of the utmost importance. Next to the corners he must be the best pass coverage man on the field.

Physical and Mental Qualifications

The ability of a pass defender to play man-for-man coverage on a receiver depends on how fast he can run. The ability to run with the man he is covering or to catch up to a receiver who has run by him is crucial. So speed is the number-one requisite in this area. However, speed is also essential in zone coverages for the free safety since it determines, to a large degree, the amount of range or ground-covering ability he has. Quickness and change of direction are critical athletic qualities he must possess to

57

DIAGRAM 7–1
Eagle Defense: The Three Deep Defenders

Normal alignment vs.
a regular two-
back formation
with corners and
free safety as the
three deep.

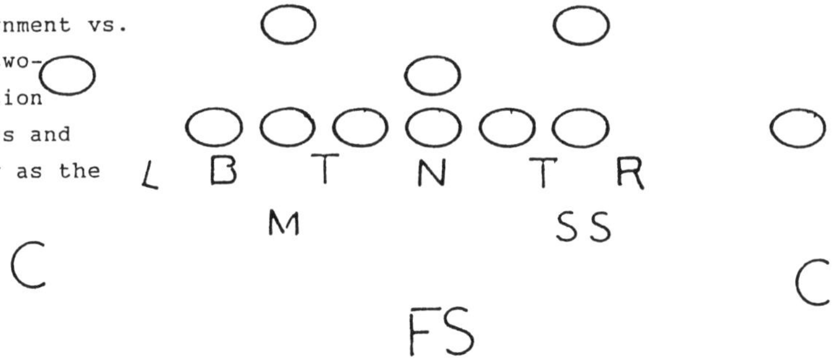

Slot formation adjustment
with corners and free safety
as the three deep defenders;
however, a normal zone rotation
vs. this formation
makes the free safety
a deep outside 1/3
defender and the inside
corner a deep middle defender.

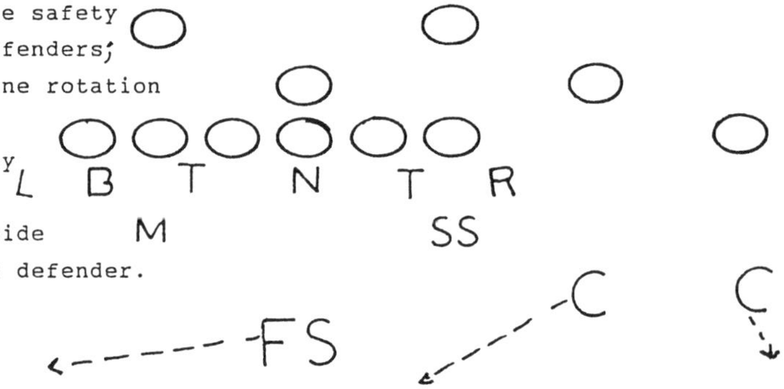

Applying the match-up theory
vs. some formations the strong safety and free safety switch positions
and the strong safety
becomes a deep middle
1/3 defender.

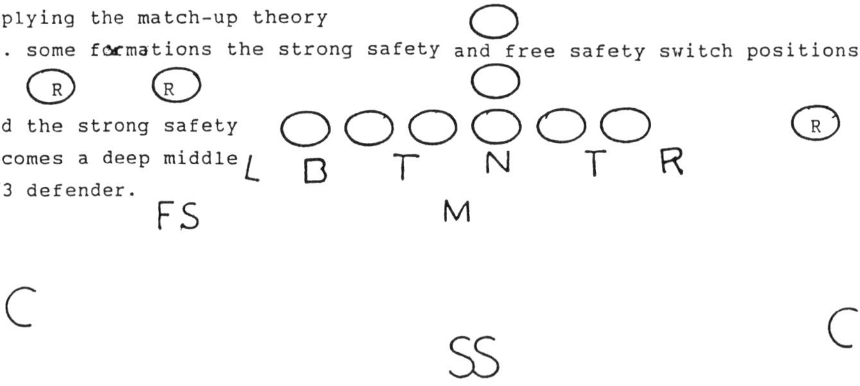

enable him to cover receivers in man coverages. These qualities are also essential in zone coverages in that they determine how well he breaks on thrown balls and reacts to receivers in his areas of responsibility. Strength is important because it allows the free safety to play the physical parts of the game well. However, strength must never be sacrificed for speed and quickness. Instinctiveness and the ability to anticipate are very necessary qualities at this position. Since the free safety spends much of his time responsible for the deep middle zone, a very large area, instinctiveness and anticipation are necessary companions of overall athletic ability. It really helps the free safety to perform to a high level if he is a knowledgeable type of football player. He really needs to be a person who is a student of the game and one who is willing to work and study to do his job well.

Alignment

The free safety lines up in the middle of the formation, 12 to 14 yards from the line of scrimmage. He must vary this alignment by stemming from a two-deep alignment, which is 14 yards deep and 2 yards inside the numbers, to his normal three-deep alignment. He should also stem to and from a position 10 to 12 yards deep over the tight end. It is important that he move around in these various alignments because from time to time he will be required to play his pass coverage in the various defenses from them. By stemming or moving around he will not give away a specific coverage when he does line up in one of these spots to play his responsibility.

Stance

The free safety should use a stance that will best enable him to cover ground. He plays in a two-point upright stance with a slight toe and heel stagger. He should have some flexion at the ankles, knees, and hips, with a small amount of weight over the balls of his feet. However, he should not have a lot of body lean forward. If he does, it negatively affects his ability to get underway and move laterally as well as backward as he reacts to execute his responsibilities.

Responsibilities

The free safety is a deep middle one-third defender in most coverages. He is expected to make plays on all balls thrown in the middle of the field. Instincts, along with his ability to key and react, will determine how much range he has or ground he can cover in this area. He is also a deep middle zone defender in the base man-for-man coverage used with the Eagle defense. If the "B" linebacker, Mac, or strong safety is used to dog or rush the passer, the free safety must replace him in coverage. He covers the tight end when the "B" linebacker is dogging; the fullback when the Mac dogs; and the H, or the number-two receiver weakside, when the strong safety dog is called.

Against the run he is a secondary run forcer on outside runs, while against inside runs he must make plays from the inside out. He is unaccounted for in most run-blocking schemes and as a result, an aggressive player in this position can be a big producer, making tackles against the run.

When coverages used with the Eagle defense are adjusted against two-back formations that have two receivers split to one side and one to the other, the free safety will cover one of the wide receivers. This is why it is very important that the free safety have the man-for-man pass coverage ability of a cornerback. When offensive teams motion to trips formation, he must be ready to assume strong safety run and pass responsibility to the strong side.

Techniques

The techniques used in playing the deep middle as a free safety are all associated with coaching the athlete who plays there so he is able to utilize his athletic skills to the utmost. Although much of what is required in the way of skills is innate or part of the makeup of the individual, coaching can develop these skills to the utmost. Reaction and movement, or the ability to cover ground, is really critical at this position. The technique of playing the deep middle starts with stance and the ability to see. He must be able to read through the offensive linemen to determine whether or not it is a run or pass play. Even though he is seeing the offensive linemen in his peripheral vision, his concentration and focus must be on the quarterback, the backfield action, and the ball. Since depth is the biggest factor in determining range, he should backpedal and get depth when he gets a pass read. Whenever he gets a run read, he should take the proper inside-out angle to make a tackle on the ball carrier. It is important that he actually see the ball handed off on runs so that he does not get fooled on a play-action pass. It is helpful, especially in teaching young free safeties, to require them to start in their backpedal each time the ball is snapped. This ensures that they will not be fooled on play-action passes.

In playing the deep middle zone, depth and the ability to take the proper angle to the ball when it is in the air are both critical to playing the position well. Depth increases range and allows the free safety to play the ball in a greater area of the field. When he reads pass and begins his backpedal, he must focus on the quarterback and the ball and pick up the receivers in his peripheral vision. If the ball is thrown in front of him, he should drive at an angle toward the line of scrimmage. Although there will be times when his angle is compromised, he must always strive to make a play on the ball in zone coverages. Catching the ball when the opportunity presents itself is crucial. When the free safety reads the quarterback and reacts well, he must make the interception by driving to the ball in front of the receiver. It is important that he strive to catch the ball in front of him at its highest point. In short, he must attack the ball. On deep balls thrown behind him he must turn and establish his angle by the flight of the ball. As he turns and runs, he must be able to turn his head and relocate the ball. While he is running and looking over his shoulder for the ball, he must continue to keep the arm working to the side at which he is looking. Unless a player concentrates on using the arm in this manner as he runs, not working the arm will slow him down in his ability to catch up to the ball. Again, he should strive to catch all balls at their highest point.

In all man-for-man coverages he uses an inside-out technique; that is, he covers the receiver by establishing and holding an inside position. It is important that he stem or move to his coverage position on the receiver just before the ball is snapped. This allows the defense to disguise dogs or blitzes as long as possible.

The technique of executing his secondary support responsibility on outside runs involves his rotating or moving to the side of the run by taking a good angle to make a play on the ball but making sure no receiver is deeper than he is. This ensures that there is no uncovered receiver who can be a primary receiver on a halfback run pass option or flea flicker play as the ball moves laterally.

Pre-snap motion by an offensive player may require that the free safety assume strong safety run and pass responsibility. As he rotates to the strong safety alignment he must place himself in a position to be a flat defender and a safety run force man in zone coverages. In man-for-man coverage he must move to an inside-out coverage position on the number-two receiver to the strong side.

CORNERS

Man-for-man pass coverage ability is the most important requisite for playing cornerback in the Eagle defense. Corners are not required, by coverage design, to be run force men very often but they are asked to cover wide receivers man-for-man on a regular basis.

Physical and Mental Qualifications

Speed is the number-one physical requisite to play the corner position well in the Eagle defense. Quickness, along with speed, enables a defender to close effectively on receivers as they run their routes. The ability to change direction effectively in conjunction with speed allows the corner to mirror or cover the receiver on his routes. All these movement qualities contribute to a player's ability to close or burst to cover a receiver when he makes his break in a pass route. The more competitive a player is, the more he will be inclined to challenge the pass receivers. This aggressive attitude is essential to success as a cornerback in this defensive scheme.

Alignment

The corner will vary his alignment from the off position to the up or the bump-and-run position. In the off position the corner lines up on the outside shoulder of the receiver seven yards off him. When the receiver lines up within six yards of the sideline, the defender applies his sideline rules and lines up on his inside shoulder. With bump and run he lines up on the line of scrimmage with a slight inside shade on the receiver. The corners flop in this defense and cover the slot man-for-man in a slot formation. They line up with a slight inside shade in either the off or the bump-and-run position. Varying these positions by moving in and out of them prior to the snap can be very effective in complicating the pre-snap read of the quarterback.

Stance

In the off position the stance of the cornerbacks should be pointed in slightly with the outside foot up. He should have a slight toe and heel stagger, with his hips and shoulder turned in slightly. This turned-in position gives the corner a broader view of the offensive formation and allows him to see all the players he needs to see, from the wide receiver on his side through the offensive linemen, backs, and the quarterback, to the ball. In the bump-and-run position he lines up in a relatively square stance with a slight inside shade on the receiver. Most players are more comfortable in a stance that has one foot slightly ahead of the other. A slight stagger is permissible but it must involve the inside foot up with the outside foot back. In all the stances the corners should have good flexion in the ankles, knees, and hips, with good body lean. It is very important that the weight distribution in his stance allow the corner to move in all directions with the same relative ease.

Responsibility

In three-deep zone defenses the corner is the deep outside one-third defender when he is lined up in his normal alignment. When he is lined up over the number-two receiver in a slot formation he is a deep middle defender. In two-deep defenses it is his responsibility to roll up, jam the outside receiver, and defend the flat-to-curl area. In man-for-man coverages it is his responsibility to cover the outside receiver on his side man-for-man. When he lines up over a slot he has coverage on him man-for-man.

Techniques

The bump-and-run technique is executed from a slight head up to slight inside position on the receiver. On the snap it is important that the corner jam the receiver with his hands. The hands should be driven at the tips of the numbers on the jersey of the receiver. It is important that the defensive man not lunge but extend his hands and arms. He is attempting to force the receiver to release outside. The outside hand should serve to impede the downfield progress of the receiver while the corner's inside hand should change his course. The jam with the inside hand should be into the arms or shoulder pad of the receiver. The corner's inside foot should always be the one closest to the line of scrimmage. The corner strives to keep the receiver from releasing inside. He should be as physical as possible with the receiver on the line of scrimmage but should not let his aggressiveness interfere with his ability to cover him.

From the off position the corner lines up seven yards off and slightly outside the receiver. When he is playing the receiver man-for-man, he must work to an inside coverage position on the receiver after the snap. If the receiver runs a pass route under the corner, he must drive on the route as soon as he reads it. If, however, the receiver is running a route up the field, the corner must backpedal and hold his original position on him. He is working for a tight outside shoulder position on the receiver. If the corner lines up inside the receiver, he backpedals, holding the inside position on routes up the field. Whether the corner plays from the bump-and-run or the off position his total concentration must be on the receiver. It is crucial that the corner learn to play the whole play. It is especially important that he be aggressive, especially on the finish, to strip the ball out of the grasp of the receiver. This is accomplished by driving down through the ball and the hands of the receiver.

In zone coverages the deep outside one-third technique used by the corner starts with an outside alignment on the receiver. On the snap, the corner starts in his backpedal. If the ball is thrown quickly in front of him, he drives on the route, putting the receiver and the ball on his inside shoulder. If the receiver drives up the field, he backpedals, holding his slight outside shoulder position on a release straight up the field. He must see the number-two receiver on his side. If both the number-one and number-two receivers are working up the field, he must place himself in a position to make a play on a ball thrown to either of the receivers. The corner must see the quarterback and the ball as he picks up the receivers in his peripheral vision. The ability to see and react to receivers in zone coverage is important. However, the issue in zone coverages is the ball; defenders must see the quarterback and the ball if they are going to make plays on the ball in zone coverages.

In two-deep zone coverages the corners are flat-to-curl defenders. Their job is to jam the wide receivers and take them out of the play and then defend the flat area. On the snap, they must move forward to jam or make contact with their hands on the receiver before he gets five yards up the field. This is an outside-in jam technique. The receiver must be prevented from a quick release downfield on the outside. As the corner jams, he tries to hit the receiver with his inside hand on his inside number. With his outside hand he makes contact with the receiver's shoulder pad or outside arm pushing to flatten his route downfield. He must read the number-two receiver on his side as well as the number-three receiver. If both the number-one and number-two receivers are releasing downfield, he must drop with the number-one receiver. If the number-three receiver runs a route in the flat and there are two upfield releasers on his side, the corner can only react up to a throw in the flat after the ball has been thrown. With only one upfield releaser on his side, the corner can jam the receiver and react more quickly to throws in the flat.

Crucial to the execution of all the skills discussed in this chapter is the ability to backpedal, react and break on a thrown ball, and be physical with the receivers on the finish. These are all techniques that can be developed and improved with repetition. The free safety and the corners all are dependent on these techniques, the perfection of which goes a long way in determining how effectively they play their positions.

8

Hawk Defense

The Hawk defense, illustrated in Diagram 8–1, was created to present a different look or alignment to the offense. This is accomplished with a minimum of position, alignment, and responsibility changes. The outside

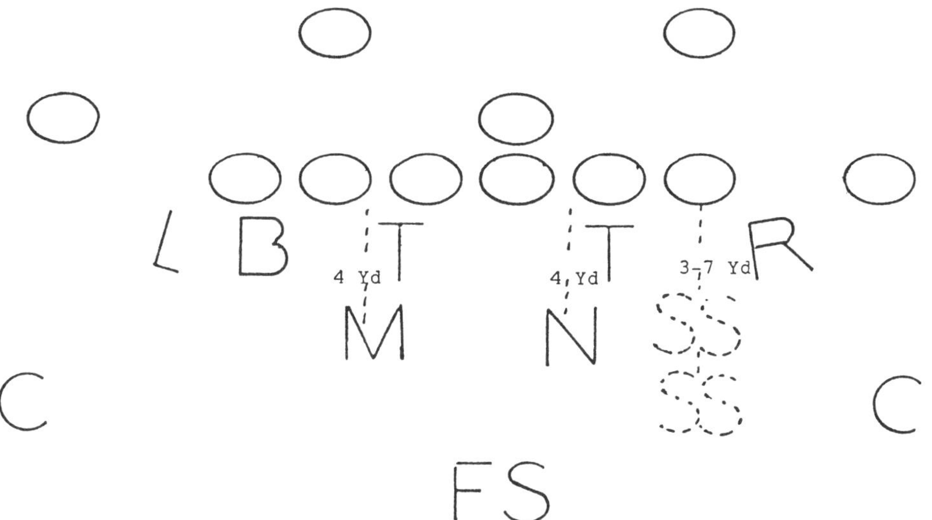

DIAGRAM 8–1
Hawk Defense

linebackers, "B" linebacker, corners, and free safety use essentially the same alignment and techniques and perform the same responsibilities as they do in the Eagle defense. The scheme is designed to create uncertainty in the minds of the blockers, especially the center, guards, and tackles. Both the run-blocking and pass-blocking schemes are affected by this look. The Hawk also creates problems for the offense since its basic design enables the nose backer to move in and out of the line of scrimmage to his stacked linebacker position. The Hawk defense also places him in a better position to play zone pass coverage than he is in, on the line of scrimmage, in the Eagle defense. Finally, the nose and Mac linebackers' stacked alignment behind the tackles places them in an advantageous position to game or stunt. Diagram 8–2 presents the Hawk defense reads and gap controls.

TACKLES

Alignment and Techniques

The normal alignment of the defensive tackles is on the outside shoulder of the offensive guard, pointed in slightly. However, one of the tackles will line up inside shade on the offensive guard or head up on him. These shades are used by the tackles in order to reduce the size of the gap between them in the middle of the defense. The Mac and the nose backer control the alignment of the tackle on their side of the defense. Generally, the rule is that the tackle to the side of an offensive formation where there is the greater outside run threat plays his normal alignment outside shade on the guard. The technique he uses is much like the one he uses in the Eagle defense. It is a hard upfield penetrating pass rush charge. He is a pass rusher and a run reactor. He is penetrating to make things happen and to distort the blocking schemes of the offense. He should see the offensive guard's action and on any pulls away from him, the tackle should continue to penetrate, flatten his route, and pursue the ball. On any plays outside his side of the formation, he should penetrate, flatten his route, and pursue the ball.

The tackle away from the run strength of the formation will get one of three calls from the Mac or nose linebacker. These calls indicate the alignment he is to use as well as the charge he is to execute. A "two-gap" call places the tackle in a head-up position on the offensive guard. This call indicates to the tackle that, on the snap of the ball, he knocks the guard back. After he has accomplished this, he is responsible for the gap to either his inside or his outside on running plays. He is responsible for the "B" gap on plays run to his side of the formation, and for the "A" gap on plays away. On pass plays he can make an inside or outside pass rush move on the

DIAGRAM 8–2
Hawk Defense Reads and Gap Controls
(Determined by Tackle Alignment and Run Reads)

Fast read strongside weak
Tackle inside
Mac - C-D Gap strong
Nose - A Gap strong
SS - B gap weak

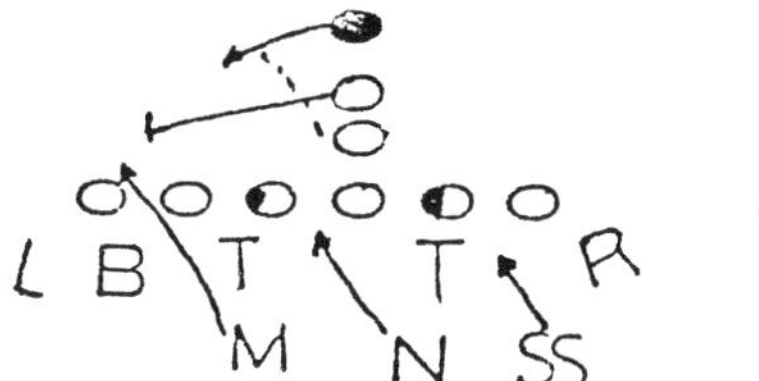

Direct read strongside weak
  Tackle inside
  Mac - A gap strongside
        outside in
  Nose - A gap strongside
        outside in
  SS - B gap weak

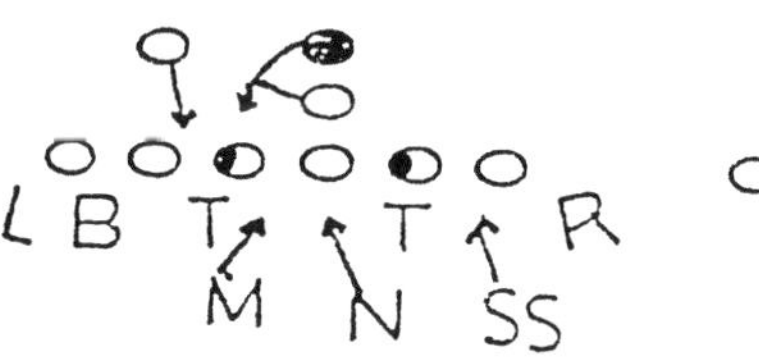

Direct read weakside weak tackle inside

  Mac - A gap strongside

  Nose - B gap weakside inside out

  SS - B gap weakside tackle

  block out - C-D gap on

  bounce out

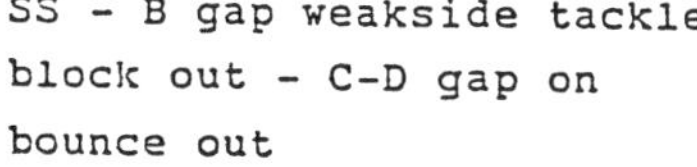
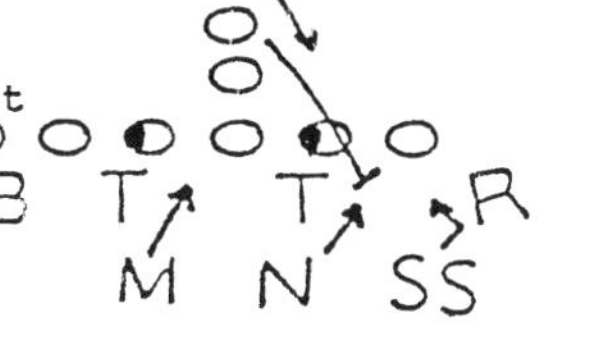

Fast read strongside strong tackle inside

Mac - C-D strongside

Nose - B gap strongside

SS - A gap weakside

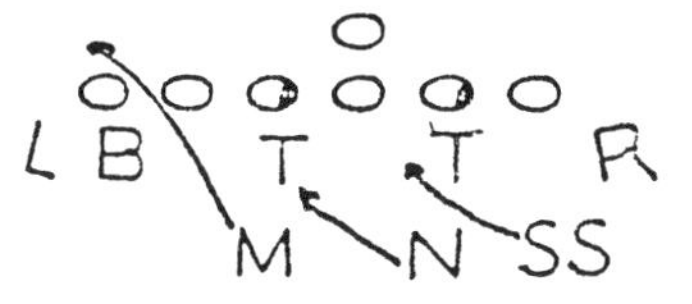

Direct read strongside strong tackle inside

Mac - B gap strongside

Nose - A gap weakside

SS - B gap weakside

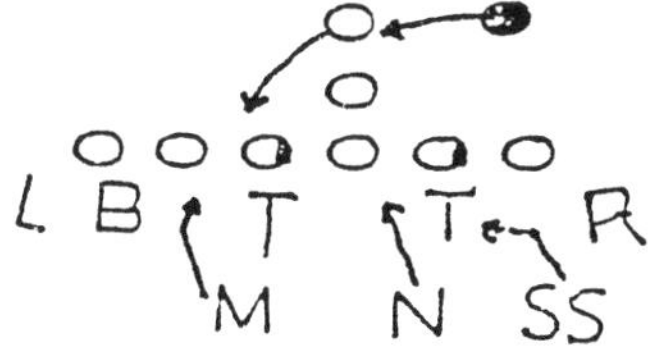

Fast read weakside strong tackle inside

  Mac - A gap

  Nose -B-C gap weakside

  SS - C-D gap weakside

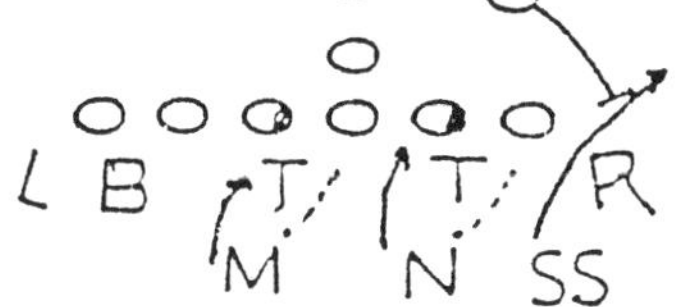

guard. With a "one" call, he stems to an inside alignment on the offensive guard, and on the snap of the ball he charges hard through the inside shoulder of the guard. With this call, the tackle is responsible for the "A" gap on all runs. He is an inside pass rusher, must penetrate up the field, and cannot be pushed or flattened down the line of scrimmage by the guard. The third call he can get is a "go" call. When the linebacker gives the tackle a go call, he is telling him to charge hard through the "A" gap. He can execute this technique by lining up in the gap or charging to the gap from a head-up alignment. Just as with a one call, his pass rush responsibility is through the "A" gap with penetration. It is important for the tackles to stem or move from one alignment to another. This stemming is useful in creating uncertainty in the minds of the offensive blockers.

MAC LINEBACKER

The Mac linebacker lines up four yards off the line of scrimmage, splitting either the inside or outside leg of the tight end-side defensive tackle. The general rule is that he lines up over the tackle's inside leg when the tackle is lined up wide. When the tackle is lined up inside or head up on the guard, Mac lines up over his outside leg. Again, the Mac controls the tackle on his side. The calls he makes to him determine the alignment and run gap responsibilities of both players. If Mac does not make any call to the tackle, he lines up in his normal wide alignment.

Responsibilities

Run

The run responsibilities of the Mac linebacker are determined by the alignment of the tackle on his side of the formation. The blocking schemes and backfield action are divided into two basic categories of reads for the Mac. One is a direct read, which is an action that involves the blockers and ball attacking the base gap responsibilities of the Mac. This is downhill action, or the type of running play where the ball is moving toward the line of scrimmage. Dives, lead plays, whams, and traps are examples of direct-read plays. The other type of action is a fast read, which involves the ball moving laterally, or across, the formation toward the perimeter to the tight-end side. End runs and off-tackle types of plays, such as sweeps, tosses, and power plays, are examples of this type of action.

On direct reads to his side of the formation, with the tackle in a normal alignment, the Mac is responsible for the strongside "A" gap. He must make these plays from the outside in putting blockers and ball on his inside shoulder pad. When the tackle is in a two-gap alignment or playing a one technique or a go call, the Mac is responsible for the "B" gap his side of the formation. On fast reads to the strong side, the Mac is responsible for the "C" to "D" gap to his side. His specific responsibility depends on the alignment of the "B" backer. Generally, if the "B" backer is lined up inside the tight end, the Mac is responsible for the "D" gap. When the "B" backer is lined up outside the tight end, Mac has primary responsibility for the "C" gap on all fast reads to his side. It is important that the Mac approach his fast-read gap responsibility with an inside-out angle. This means that regardless of whether he is responsible for the "C" or "D" gap, he must take a good downhill inside-out angle to the ball. He should avoid a head-up position on any ball carrier since this places him in a position where he would be vulnerable to overrunning the ball. He must apply the principle of always taking something away from the ball carrier by his pursuit angle to the ball. Again, by working downhill and inside out to the ball carrier, he limits his options. With the Mac's position on the ball carrier taking away the inside cut, he has only one way to go and that is outside. This makes tackling the ball carrier a reasonable expectation.

On direct reads to the weak side of the formation, the Mac is responsible for the "A" gap strongside when the tackle strongside is lined up in his normal wide alignment. When his tackle is in any of the other alignments, the Mac is responsible for the "B" gap strongside if the ball is run there on a cutback play. He may start to move toward the weak side on any of these types of plays and continue to the ball if it stays on that side. However, if the ball carrier does cut back in the "B" gap, the Mac must be a factor on that play. On any fast read weakside, the Mac should take a good inside-out pursuit angle to the ball.

Pass

The Mac has the same pass responsibilities in the Hawk defense that he has in the Eagle defense. He is responsible for the F, or the number-three receiver strongside in most man-for-man coverages. He can use an in-and-out call with the "B" backer, just as he does in the Eagle. In most zone coverages he is a strongside hook-to-curl defender exactly like he is in the Eagle defense.

NOSE LINEBACKER

The nose linebacker lines up four yards off the line of scrimmage opposite the "A" gap, or the gap between the center and the weakside guard. He lines up in this position against all two-back offensive sets. This alignment is constant as long as the strong safety is lined up in his normal position over the weakside offensive tackle. When the strong safety vacates this position, as he does against one-back formations, and when a two-deep zone coverage has been called, the nose linebacker must adjust accordingly. Against one-back formations, the nose linebacker will line up according to the alignment of his offensive tackle. He applies the same general rules the Mac does for lining up his tackle in the proper position. He will stack over the inside or outside leg of the defensive tackle on his side. If the tackle is lined up in a two-gap or a one alignment, the nose will stack over his outside leg. If the tackle does not get a call, he lines up in the "B" gap and the Mac lines up over his inside leg. The run strength of the formation determines the alignment the nose linebacker places the tackle in. In any formation that is basically a running formation, the weakside tackle will not get a call. That means he will line up in his normal wide alignment and be responsible for the "B" gap. Against strongside run formations the nose linebacker will give his tackle a one, two-gap, or go call. It is very important that the nose linebacker not adjust according to his tackle's alignment against two-back formations. Against two-back formations, the nose linebacker lines up over the weakside "A" gap.

Responsibilities

Run

The nose linebacker has the same system of direct and fast reads that Mac has. With his tackle normal and a direct read, the nose linebacker is responsible for the "A" gap to his side. If he gives the tackle a one, two-gap, or go call, he is responsible for the "B" gap on any direct read. On fast reads to his side of the formation the nose works through the "B" to the "C" to the "D" gap. He must always work inside out and up and in to the ball.

On direct reads to the strong side of the formation the nose linebacker will be responsible for the strongside "A" gap when the weakside tackle is lined up in his normal alignment. On strongside runs whenever the weakside tackle is, by his alignment, assigned the weakside "A" gap, the nose linebacker is responsible for the strongside "A" gap. On fast reads to the strong side he should take a good inside-out pursuit angle to the ball.

Pass

The nose linebacker is a weakside hook-to-curl defender in most zone coverages. He is a weakside curl-to-flat defender against trips formations. In man coverages he is a pass rusher and will usually run a stunt or game with his tackle.

STRONG SAFETY

The strong safety plays with the same run and pass responsibilities that he has in the Eagle defense. However, he does line up wider against some two-back formations. His rule is that he lines up on the outside shoulder of the offensive tackle. If he lines up head up on the tackle, he and the nose linebacker will be too close to each other. This adjustment gives both players room to operate without crowding each other. It is also important, against any two-back set where there is a halfback lined up to his side, that he line up clearly outside the back. He cannot allow the tackle or back on the weak side of the formation to establish an outside blocking position on him.

All remaining players line up and execute their responsibilities just as they do in the Eagle defense.

9

Teaching the Defense: Drills and Techniques

I have always believed that any coach can go to the chalkboard and draw a particular defensive scheme. However, I feel it takes skilled people who are good teachers to coach a scheme effectively. Knowing what to teach is one thing but knowing how to teach it is something else. In my opinion, too many coaches spend too much of their time trying to outscheme or outcoach their opponents and not enough time developing ways to teach skills to their players. This chapter presents ways to teach players the skills necessary to play the Eagle defense effectively.

At the root of outexecuting the opponent's offense is the acquisition of sound techniques by the defensive players. I believe that each position on a team has two or three important techniques to be mastered. The skilled position coach has the responsibility to define these crucial skills and find ways to teach them. If there are a limited number of techniques or skills taught, a player has a chance to perfect them by repetition. If however, large numbers of different kinds of techniques are taught, there is a very good chance the player will not be able to execute any of them well. The average skilled player usually becomes a great player or overachiever due to intensity and the perfection of techniques. The player with high levels of ability achieves more and becomes a more consistent player as he acquires techniques.

It is the coaches' responsibility to motivate players and teach techniques. Too many coaches see themselves as great tacticians and spend too little time and effort motivating and teaching. The best position coaches I know are exceptional teachers of technique. They know what they want to teach and how they want to teach it. They set high standards and expectations for the execution of techniques and demand that their players try to achieve them. They are good at teaching the two or three techniques that are the most crucial in playing the particular position they coach. These coaches also have the ability to convince the players they coach of the importance of technique as it relates to consistency in performance. I have always believed that good technique players can play every play and every game well. Techniques are at the very foundation of consistency. If a player is really good at what he does it does not matter what the opponent does. I have always believed that the primary objective of the defensive team is to keep the opponent from scoring. The defense accomplishes this by outexecuting the opponents' offense with techniques.

Drills are used by coaches to teach techniques. Some drills are conducted "on air," that is, without any opponent players, dummies, sleds, or other devices. These drills are the type that are used to teach any type of movement, such as takeoff, to defensive linemen, up-and-in angles to linebackers, and backpedaling to defensive backs. There are also drills that utilize devices like dummies or cones. These types of devices are used to teach gap responsibilities, pass rush lanes, and zone drop areas. Drills that utilize dummies mounted on platforms or sleds are used to teach hand use, striking a blow, and tackling to defensive players. There are three basic types of line drills, or drills that utilize opponent-type players. These line drills are divided into three basic types—one-on-one, group or segment, and team drills.

Logical progressions of the line drills can be developed for most defensive schemes. With one-on-one drills, teaching is accomplished best by progressing from a slow pace or walking tempo to half speed, and slowly moving to offensive and defensive players' competing at full speed. After each player has been exposed to the individual techniques at his position, groups of players are brought together for segment drills. These group, or segment, drills are designed to bring parts of the defense together for specific teaching. These drills basically teach players how they are to work together in a defensive scheme. They are essential because a specific portion of the defense can be taught specific skills needed to play that part of the defense well. At the same time other groups of players can be working together on techniques unique to their segment of the defense. Examples of these types of drills are half-side drills where one-half side of the defense works against one-half side of the offense. This would involve a nose tackle, defensive tackle, "B" linebacker, outside linebacker, and Mac working against a center, offensive guard, tackle, tight end, quarterback, and two running backs. Another example of a functional segment, or group, drill is the five-on-three drill where the two defensive tackles and the nose linebacker work against the offensive tackles, guards, and center.

Every drill must have specific objectives. Assigning drills for drill's sake makes no sense to me.

OUTSIDE LINEBACKERS

Outside Linebacker Takeoff Drill (Diagram 9—1)

Since the basic design of the Eagle defense is to feature the outside linebackers as pass rushers, takeoff is where their training must start. The development of takeoff, or initial quickness, is the basic objective of this drill. In addition to speed, elevation is an important part of this technique. The ability to gain distance up the field and not raise up out of the stance

DIAGRAM 9—1
Outside Linebacker Takeoff Drill

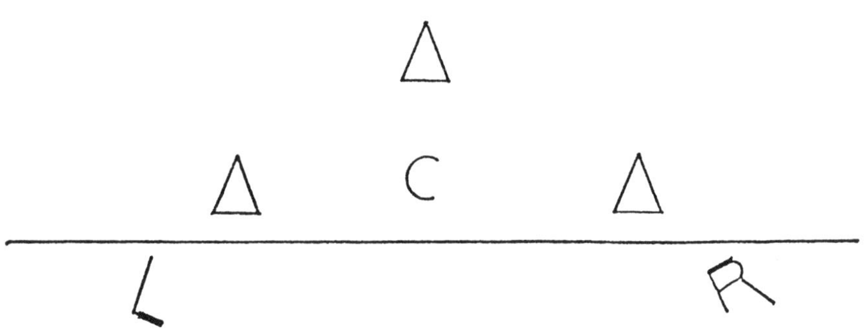

C – Coach uses varied cadence and snaps football.

L & R – In normal stance, pointed in slightly – aiming point is four yards deep directly behind offensive center. Position normally occupied by an offensive fullback.

△ – Cones or dummies used to represent the position normally occupied by the offensive tight end, tackles and fullback.

——— – Yardline on football field or sideline. Important for alignment.

must be developed and monitored with this drill. The angle the linebackers rush should also be coached with this drill. This angle should be a straight line toward the position normally occupied by the fullback; that is, about four yards deep in the backfield at a point directly behind the center. This simple drill can be used when players are practicing with or without pads. It is a very good off-season drill for the teaching of takeoff, elevation, and angles of rush.

Outside Linebacker One-on-One Blocks, Tight-End Side (Diagram 9–2)

The outside linebacker must react to and defeat one-on-one or single blocks by several different offensive players. He must read and react to the running play blocks as he rushes the passer. The ability to adjust his angle to the various blocks is a skill he must master. The best way to begin teaching this reaction is to place offensive players in their various positions and have them block the outside linebacker as he rushes the passer. These reactions to run blocks as he rushes hard upfield must be repeated over and over again. If he sees enough of these types of blocks, he will become more skilled at reacting to them. He will also gain confidence in his ability to rush the passer with great velocity and yet be able to successfully execute his run responsibility. The outside linebacker must squeeze all run blocks from the outside in when he is the force man. If he is not the force man, he can two-gap or make an inside move on the blocker. The linebacker can make an inside move on a run blocker only if he is making his move on him up the field or in the opponent's backfield. Since he is an outside pass rusher and he must keep the quarterback inside, most of the time he will rush over the outside of pass blockers. However, he must have the latitude to go to the inside or to make inside moves on blockers whenever he has an opportunity to get to the quarterback using this technique.

Outside Linebacker One-on-One Blocks, Open Side (Diagram 9–3)

The open-side linebacker reacts to the various blocks the same way as does the linebacker on the tight-end side. Since there is no tight end to his side he lines up closer to the blockers who will block him. This means the blockers will get to him sooner, forcing a quicker reaction to their blocks. He must therefore be able to adjust his angles more quickly without slowing down his pass rush. Lining up wider and pointing in at a sharper angle helps him adjust his pass rush to react better to these blocks.

DIAGRAM 9–2
Outside Linebacker One-on-One Blocks, Tight-End Side

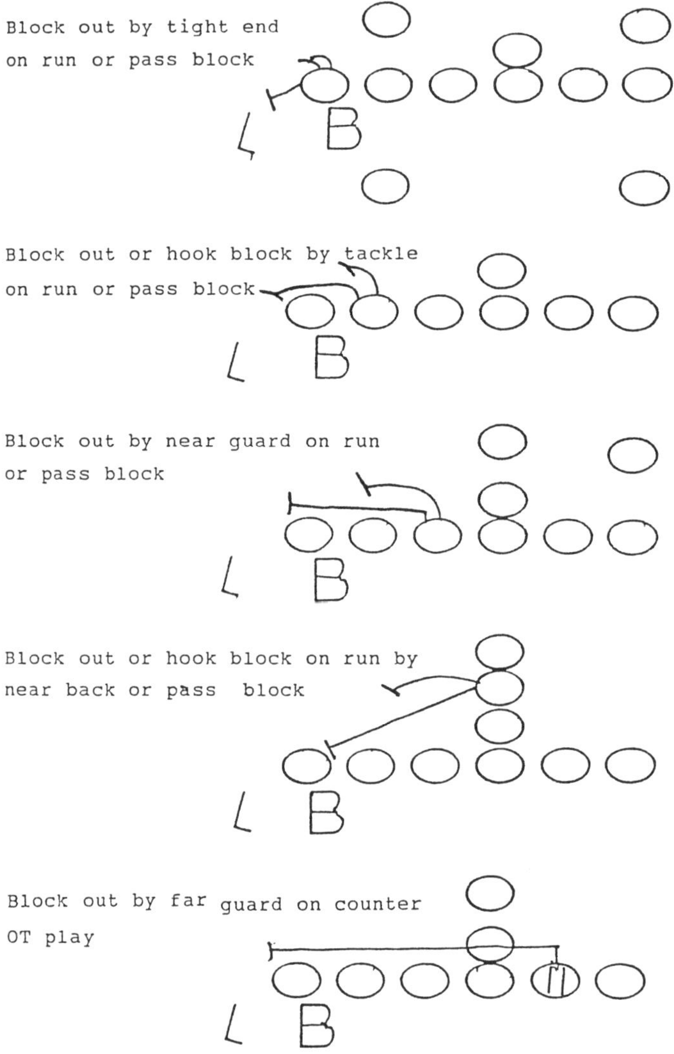

Note: On all blocks above, outside linebacker squeezes or compresses cutback lane and holds outside force position, bounces the ball deep or makes the tackle. On passes, he is the outside rusher on his side. He has the latitude to make inside moves when quarterback is stepping up in the pocket.

DIAGRAM 9–3
Outside Linebacker One-on-One Blocks, Open Side

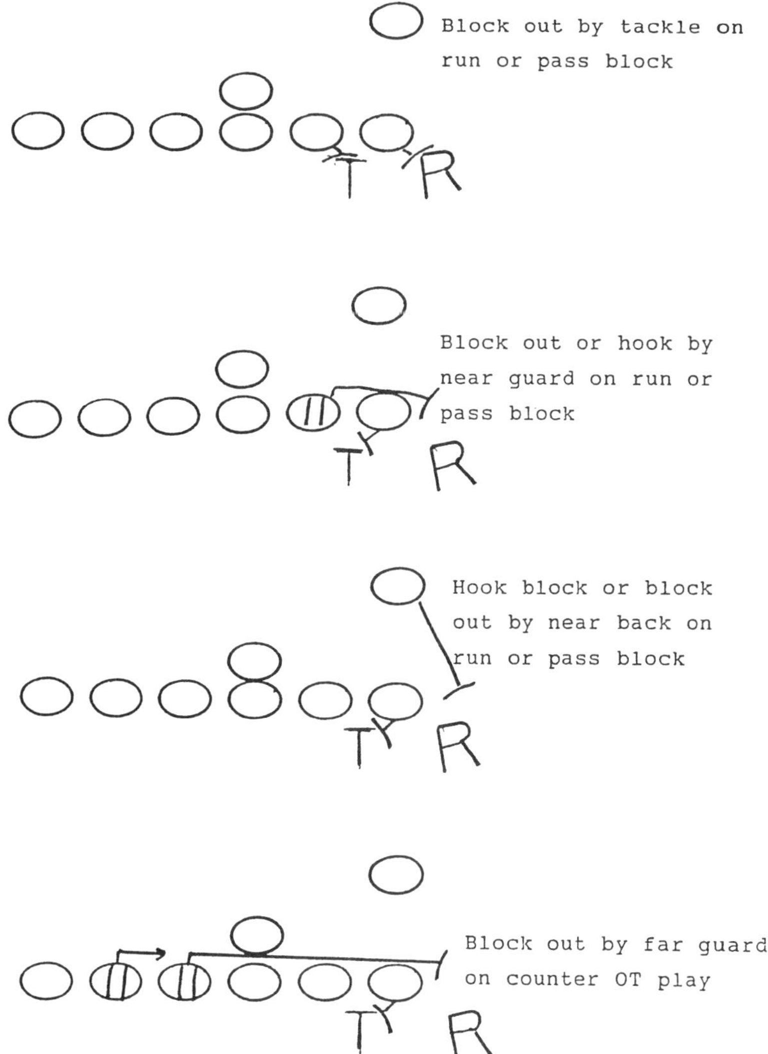

Note: On all blocks above, outside linebacker squeezes or compresses cutback lane and holds outside force position, bounces the ball deep or makes the tackle. On passes, he is the outside rusher on his side. He has the latitude to make inside moves when the quarterback steps up in the pocket.

DIAGRAM 9–4
"B" Linebacker One-on-One Blocks

Down block by tight
end on outside runs

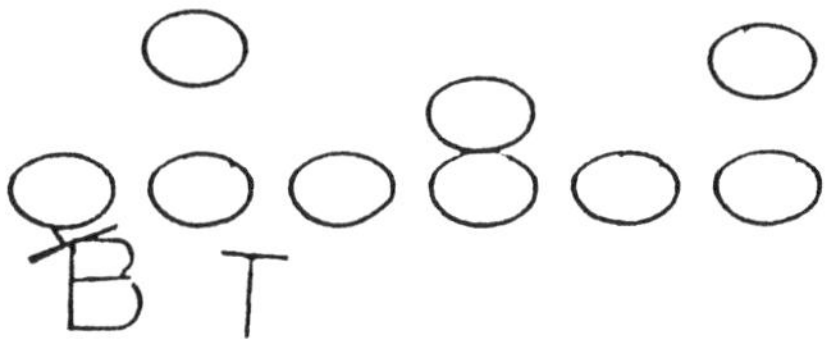

Influence block by tight end
and block out by guard

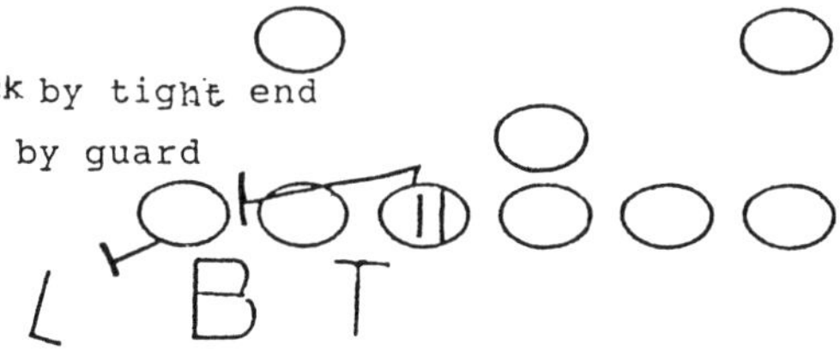

Influence block by tight end
and block out by near back

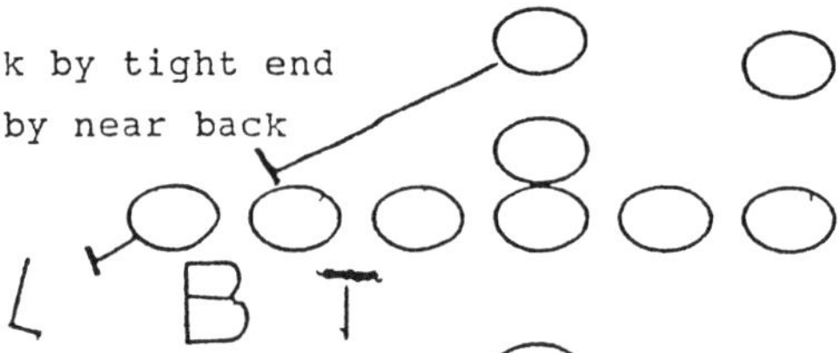

Influence block by tight end and
block out by far guard on counter
OT play

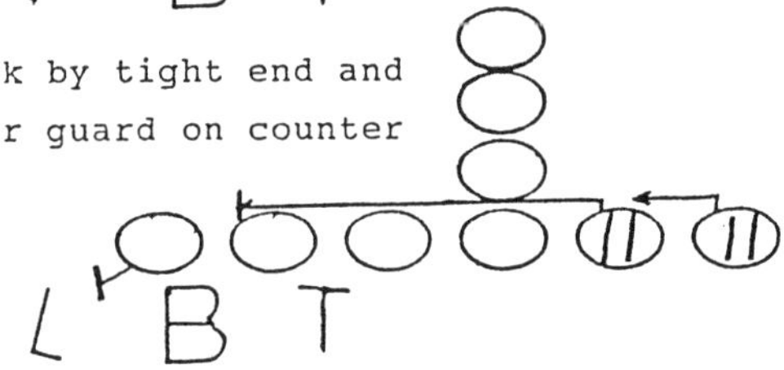

Pass block by guard when B
linebacker is dogging in A
gap

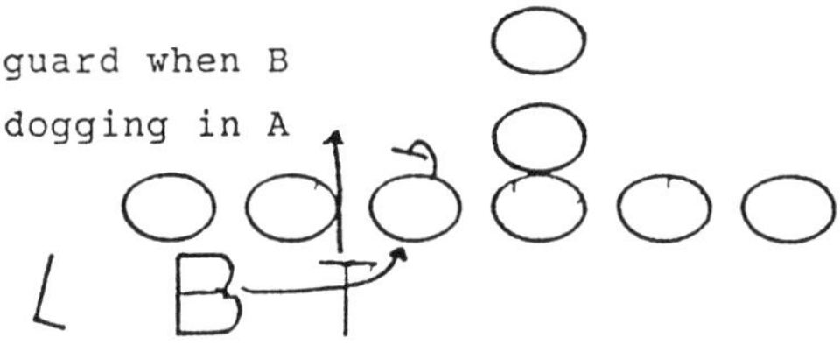

Out block by tight end when
tight end is in outside alignment
to play in-and-out
coverage with
Mac

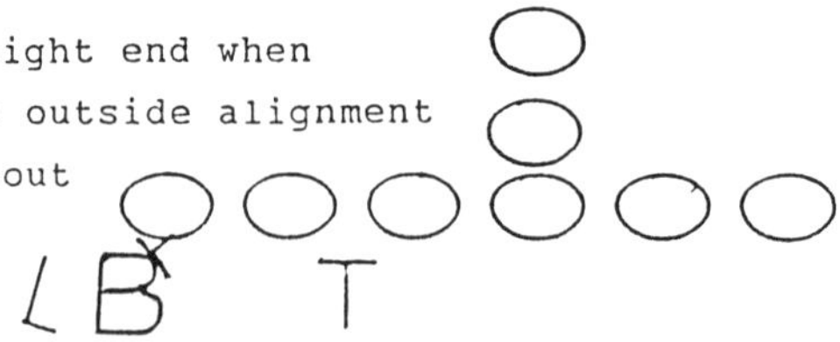

"B" Linebacker One-on-One Blocks
(Diagram 9—4)

The "B" linebacker must learn to defeat one-on-one blocks by the tight end. When he is lined up inside the tight end, he must work the tight end upfield and hold the "C" gap. When he is lined up outside the tight end, he must squeeze his block, closing the "C" gap with the blocker while he holds his "D" gap responsibility. Blocks by players other than the tight end attack the "B" backer from the inside. The tight end fakes a block on him or influences him and then either of the guards or a running back blocks out. He must feel the influence of the tight end, look inside, and attack the blockers squeezing, or compressing, the hole with them as he holds his "C" gap responsibility.

When he is dogging or blitzing as a pass rusher, the "B" linebacker can make an inside or outside move on the tackle when he blocks him. The general rule is that he must beat the tackle quickly on an outside rush; if he doesn't, he must make an inside move on him. If he doesn't do this, he will be pushed outside by the offensive tackle into the rush lane of the outside linebacker. When he rushes over the guard, as he does in some games, he can make an inside or outside move on him.

TACKLES

Tackles' Takeoff Drill
(Diagram 9—5)

The tackles must be taught the proper elements of takeoff, or initial quickness. The best way to do this is to use the tackles' takeoff drill. The drill is set up on a yard line on a football field in order to best monitor the alignment as well as the quickness of the tackles in their takeoff. Cones or dummies are used to represent offensive guards, and they are placed about five yards apart. A coach or manager is used as a center to snap the ball, with a player, coach, or manager lined up in the fullback position to indicate pass or run to the right or left. The coach should use various kinds of cadence in order to get the player accustomed to concentrating on the movement of the ball or man and not on the voice inflections of the quarterback. On movement, the tackles charge low and hard across the line of scrimmage and react to the action of the person in the fullback position. If he simulates pass, they should continue upfield and rush the passer. If he moves to the right or left, they should flatten their route and work to get in front of the ball carrier. Quickness and elevation in takeoff

DIAGRAM 9–5
Tackles' Takeoff Drill

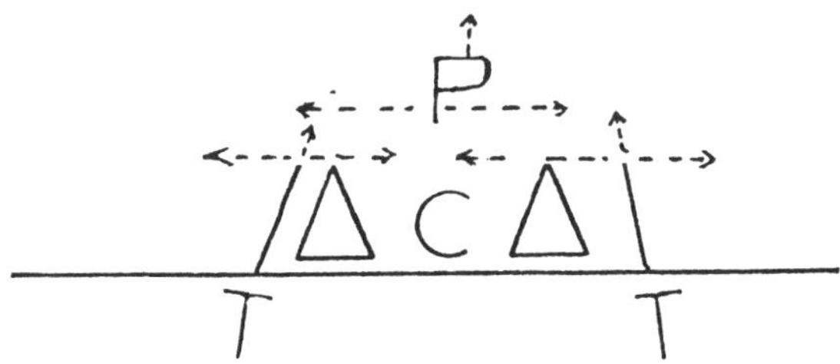

C – Coach uses varied cadences and snaps football.

T – Tackles in normal stance and alignment slightly pointed in.
On movement, penetrate and react to movement of player represented
by symbol behind C. Tackles will react flat right or left or
continue upfield rushing passer if pass is indicated by person
in deep position.

△ – Cones or dummies used to represent guards.

P – Player, manager or coach to indicate run right or left or pass.

as well as the ability to pass rush and flatten their routes against runs are
all developed in this drill.

Tackles' One-on-One Blocks
(Diagram 9–6)

The tackles' one-on-one blocks drill requires two players to simulate
an offensive guard and tackle on each side of the defense. Both tackles can
work at the same time. The coach indicates the type of block he wants the
offensive players to execute, and the defensive tackles work to develop the
proper reaction. With a down block by the offensive tackle they should
penetrate, flatten their route, and pursue outside on the offensive side of
the line of scrimmage. With a base or reach-block by the guard the tackles
should beat the block by the guard and squeeze on inside plays, and flatten
and pursue on outside plays. On a pass block by the guard the tackle
should first try to beat the guard upfield and outside. If he cannot, he
should make an inside move on the guard in order to not be pushed into
R's or L's outside pass rush lane.

DIAGRAM 9–6
Tackles' One-on-One Blocks

Down block by tackle
outside run or pass block

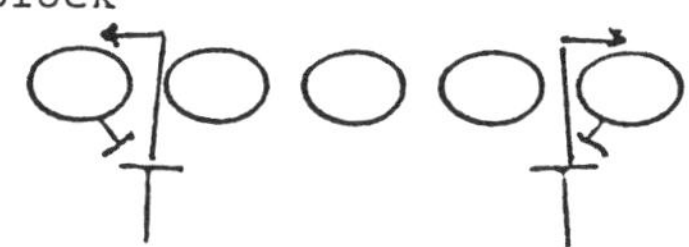

Base block or reach
block by guard on run

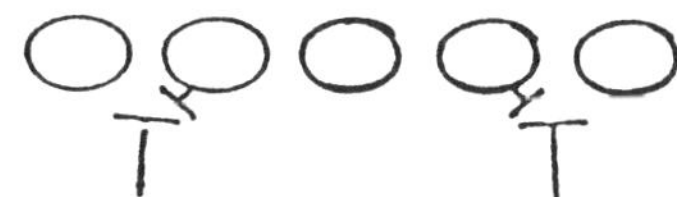

Pass block by guard
drop back or play-action
pass

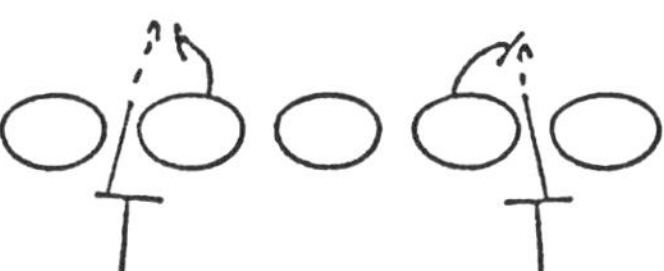

Note: Down block by tackle, want tackle to penetrate, flatten route
    and pursue outside on offensive side of the line of scrimmage.
- Base block or reach block by guard, want tackle to hold B gap
  and squeeze A gap with guard. Work for penetration.
- Pass block by guard, rush B gap lane – careful not to get pushed
  out into R or L rush lane – if do not beat guard upfield
  can make inside rush move on guard.

Tackles' Two-on-One Base Blocks
(Diagram 9–7)

The same offensive personnel are used as in the tackles' one-on-one
drill. This drill teaches the tackles how to play off the various types of
blocks that start as combination blocks by the guard and tackle. The tackle
must be taught that it is crucial that he maintain control of the "B" gap on
every type of combination block. He cannot be pushed by one player into a
single block by the other player that takes away his control of the "B" gap.
On a solid double-team block by both the guard and tackle he must hold
his ground and not be knocked back into the Mac or strong safety.

DIAGRAM 9–7
Tackles' Two-on-One Base Blocks

Double push with tackle and
guard double-teaming tackle
and either trying to push him
back into Mac and the strong
safety. Or the guard or
tackle coming off on Mac
or the strong safety after
they start movement back on
the tackle.

Guard and tackle combo block
on outside run. Tackle and guard
are responsible for tackle
and Mac on strong side and
tackle and Strong Safety on
weak side.

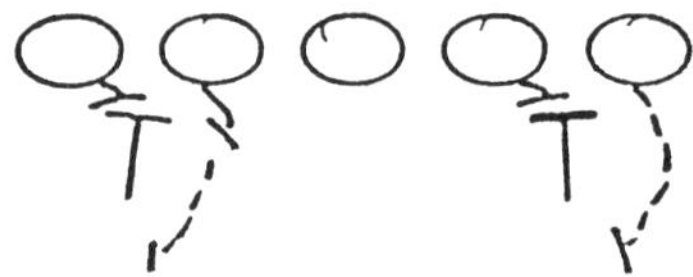

Note: Critical that on all forms of 2-on-1 or combo
blocks, tackle maintains control of the B gap.

Nose Three-on-One Basic Blocks
(Diagram 9–8)

The nose tackle faces blocking threats from the center or either
guard on every play. This drill gives the nose the opportunity to work
against these combinations. Defensive players are used to simulate the
center and two guards. The center blocks the nose alone, which allows him

to work on his two-gap technique. Or, the center works in concert with one of the guards, executing a combo or scoop block. The nose must work to hold the "A" gap to the side of the block and not let the center take away the "A" gap. He must work upfield or toward the offensive side of the line of scrimmage as he plays through these blocking combinations.

DIAGRAM 9—8
Nose Three-on-One Basic Blocks

Center base or man block
when nose is using two-gap
technique - pass or run.

Center and guard combo block on nose – Nose must work to front side
or play side gap unless call gives him backside gap responsibility,
he then must maintain
backside A gap control.

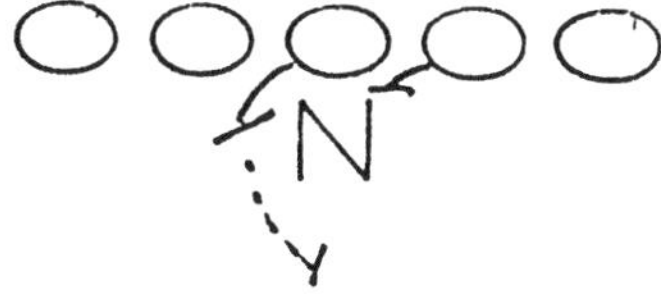

Note: Important that nose works up the field or toward the
offensive line of scrimmage as he works through the blockers to
his base gap responsibility

Five-on-Three Combination Base Blocks (Diagram 9–9)

This drill essentially combines all the elements of the tackles' one-on-one blocks, tackles' two-on-one blocks, and the nose three-on-one basic blocks. All the combinations described in the previous drills are used. This drill is essential in that it forces the defensive players to react on a broader

DIAGRAM 9–9
Five-on-Three Combination Base Blocks

Nose single-blocked by center

and double-push combo block by
guards and tackles on defensive tackles.

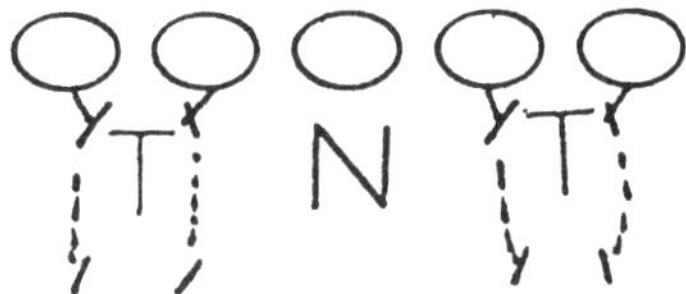

Combo block on tackle by guard and tackle to the side of
the play with a combo block by the center and backside guard
on the nose. Cutoff block on the backside tackle by the offensive
tackle.

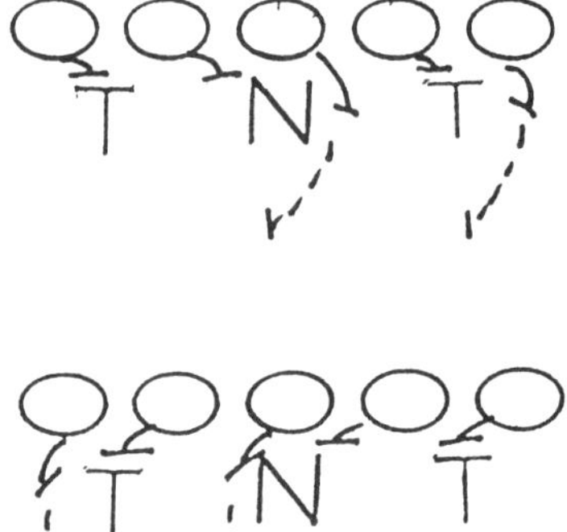

Note: It is very important that these combinations of
blocks are used in conjunction with the teaching of the scheme
in its early stages and continued on a regular basis. It is
also important that the three defensive players are coached to
work up the field or toward the offensive line of scrimmage
as they maintain their gap control.

scale. Since more offensive players are involved, this drill works out to present excellent opportunities for reactions to various offensive schemes. The availability of a running back helps to make this a more functional drill. With a back to establish the direction of a play, a more specific reaction by the defensive players can be demanded on each play.

MAC AND STRONG SAFETY
BASIC TECHNIQUE DRILLS

The progression of technique teaching for these players should start on a blocking sled. The hands technique so critical in defeating blockers is best taught initially on these devices. The normal progression takes them from the sleds, to one-on-one working against other defensive players, to working against offensive blockers. It is important that the hands technique be taught as a means to defeat blockers. However, the proper emphasis must be given to the hands as a means to gain operating space and accelerate off blocks to the ball carrier. Again, the proper progression of technique should carry through to include these areas.

Mac and Strong Safety Gap Control
Cone Drill (Diagram 9–10)

The cone drill teaches the Mac and strong safety their base gap responsibilities against the run. They each have a series of reads that tells them exactly what their gap responsibilities are. A direct read tells them that the ball and blockers are attacking them straight ahead. A fast read tells them that the ball is attacking the perimeter to their side. A slow-read play tells them that there is a chance the ball will start in one direction away from them, either counter or cutback to their side.

This drill uses five cones, set approximately $1\frac{1}{2}$ yards apart. The coach lines up behind the center cone five yards from the line of scrimmage. The coach simulates the action of the running back as he runs a specific backfield action. It is best that the coach begin the drill by running the drill as a one-step drill. That is, he takes one step in the direction of the play he is to run. The Mac and strong safety are expected to mirror these steps. After they have one-stepped these actions to the point where they are not taking any false steps, the coach can finish the action of the back.

In this drill the footwork, shoulder level, and up-and-in actions of the defensive men should be monitored in addition to teaching specific gap responsibilities according to backfield action.

DIAGRAM 9–10
Mac and Strong Safety Gap Control Cone Drill

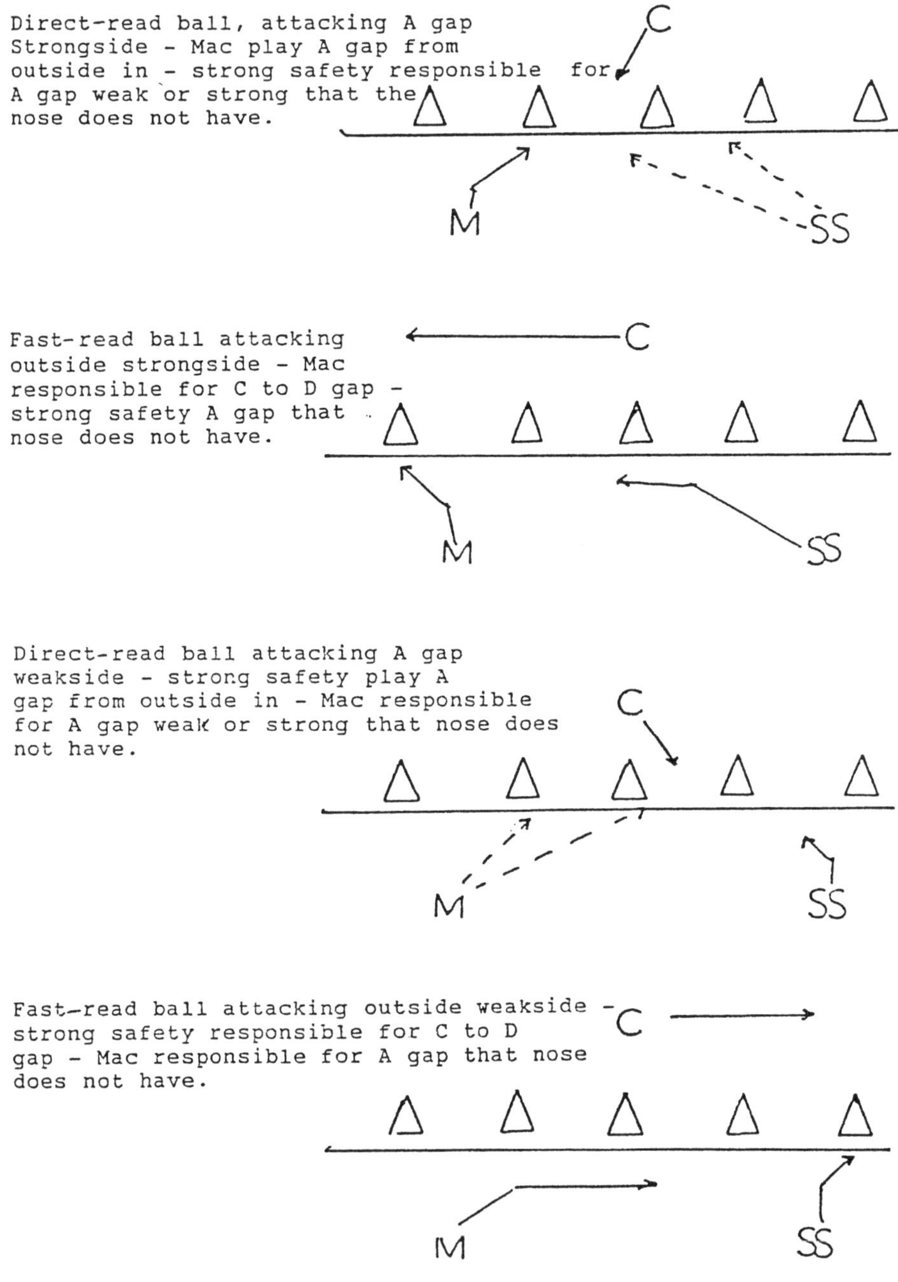

Direct-read ball, attacking A gap Strongside - Mac play A gap from outside in - strong safety responsible for A gap weak or strong that the nose does not have.

Fast-read ball attacking outside strongside - Mac responsible for C to D gap - strong safety A gap that nose does not have.

Direct-read ball attacking A gap weakside - strong safety play A gap from outside in - Mac responsible for A gap weak or strong that nose does not have.

Fast-read ball attacking outside weakside - strong safety responsible for C to D gap - Mac responsible for A gap that nose does not have.

Mac and Strong Safety Zone Pass Drops
(Diagram 9–11)

Mac

The Mac and the strong safety drop on movement of the ball by the coach who is approximately eight yards away, facing them. Mac is a hook-to-curl defender. On movement by the coach he starts his drop at approximately a 45-degree angle. He should keep his shoulder level the same as it was in his stance all the way through his drop. He should open with his hips and shoulders as parallel as possible to the line of scrimmage. As he drops he needs to be able to react to a QB three-step drop.

It is important not to raise the shoulder level all through the drop. If Mac keeps his shoulder level down, his weight will be distributed over the balls of his feet thus enabling him to break to the ball on the look and throw of the quarterback. Mac's angle of drop is usually determined by the pass release of the number-two receiver to his side of the formation. On the strong side of the formation it is usually the tight end, and on the weak side it is usually the back.

The coach drops straight back, keeping his shoulder parallel with the line of scrimmage and looking straight ahead. As the player goes to his hook drop he must look back to the coach for three-step drop. If the coach shows a three-step drop, Mac must drive in the direction of the coach's action. If the coach continues to drop, Mac also continues in his drop. He continues to get depth until the coach gives him a direction by turning his shoulders and starting a throwing action. When this happens, Mac drives to the ball and catches the thrower's ball. Mac should drive toward the line of scrimmage at about a 45-degree angle. The normal drop should be about 10 to 12 yards deep, at about a 45-degree angle. This angle changes according to the release of the number-two receiver.

Strong Safety

The strong safety is a curl-to-flat defender. He too must keep his shoulder level constant from his initial stance all through the actual drop. His aiming point is just inside the numbers on an NFL field, about 10 to 12 yards deep. His drop is at approximately a 60-degree angle. He too must keep his head on a swivel and react to a three-step drop by the quarterback in the same fashion that the Mac does.

It is important that both the Mac and the strong safety become proficient at reading the look and throw of the quarterback. They are short defenders in the zone coverages and therefore must be able to get a quick jump on balls thrown in their area. This drill helps them develop these techniques.

DIAGRAM 9–11
Mac and Strong Safety Zone Pass Drops

Mac start hook – curl drop and strong
safety start curl – flat drop – read
3-step drop by quarterback and break
flat in direction of throw. Right or
left.

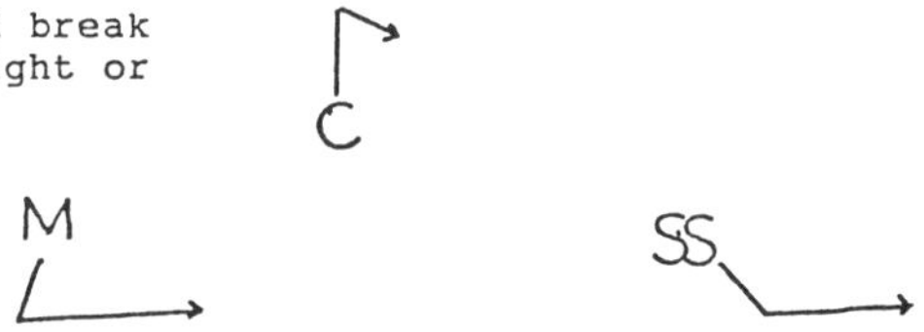

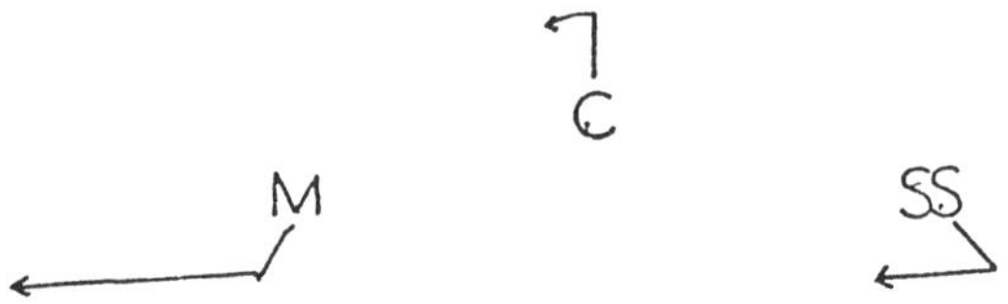

Start their zone drop and break
on look and throw of quarterback.
Right or left.

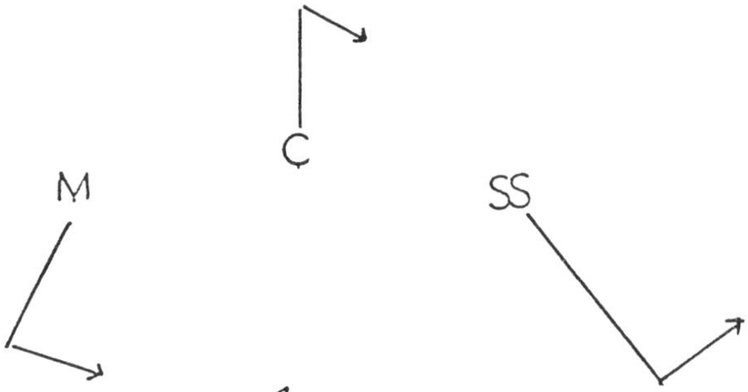

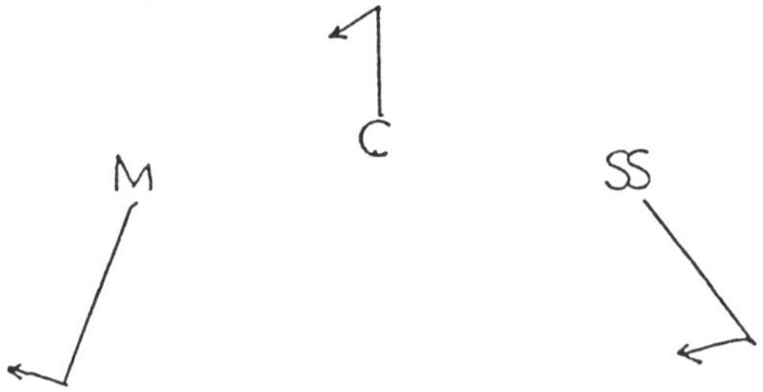

Note: It is important that Mac and strong safety start their
pass drop, then get their eyes back on the quarterback and break in
the direction the quarterback looks and throws. Coach acts as QB
and takes 3 step or 5 step and turns his shoulder to give direction.

Mac and Strong Safety Man-for-Man Coverage (Diagram 9–12)

The Mac and the strong safety line up about eight yards off and slightly inside the back on their side. The coach stands behind the defenders and signals the pass routes he wants the backs to run. An inside-

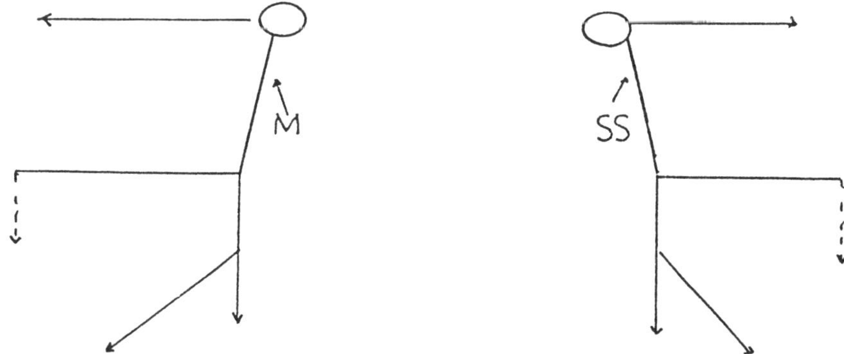

DIAGRAM 9–12
Mac and Strong Safety Man-for-Man Coverage

out catch technique is used. On the snap of the ball, both the Mac and the strong safety start toward the man they are covering, concentrating on the hips or belt buckle of the receiver. All coverages are from the inside out; in other words, the defender cannot allow the receiver inside. It is a trail technique on deep balls. It is important that the defender be as physical as possible when he catches or junctions the receiver he is approaching. If the receiver tries to release across the middle, he should jam him into the line of scrimmage. As with all man-for-man coverage defenders, it is important to compete through the whistle. It is also important that the defender concentrate on the hands of the receiver or the pocket he makes with them to catch the ball. He should not look back at the quarterback when covering in a man-for-man situation. He should work to strip the ball from the receiver as he catches it. It is good technique to try to get the ball away from the receiver until the whistle blows.

Corners and Free Safety One-on-One Pass Coverage (Diagram 9—13)

This drill involves the corners and free safety working against wide receivers and a quarterback. The players work from either the bump or press position or the off position head up on the receiver about seven yards deep. It is also desirable to work from a slight outside shade position from the off alignment.

Press position.   It is very important that the defender get his hands on the receiver when working from this position. His aiming point is the outside tips of the numbers on the front of the receiver's jersey. The objective is to disrupt his upfield release—to change his release angle. The defender can never let the receiver off on a clean inside release. If the receiver attempts to release inside, the defender should flatten the receiver route by jamming him on the line of scrimmage.

Off position.   When executing this drill the defender lines up head up or slightly outside the receiver. On the snap he works an inside position on the receiver. He should work for a position on the inside hip of the receiver with full concentration on the receiver until he reaches for the ball. When the receiver reaches for the ball, the defender should position himself between the receiver and the ball, look for the ball, and make a play on it.

It is very important that defenders be taught to play the whole play. They must compete until the whistle blows. The defender must work to strip the ball whenever a receiver catches it on every play in practice.

DIAGRAM 9–13
Corners and Free Safety One-on-One Pass Coverage

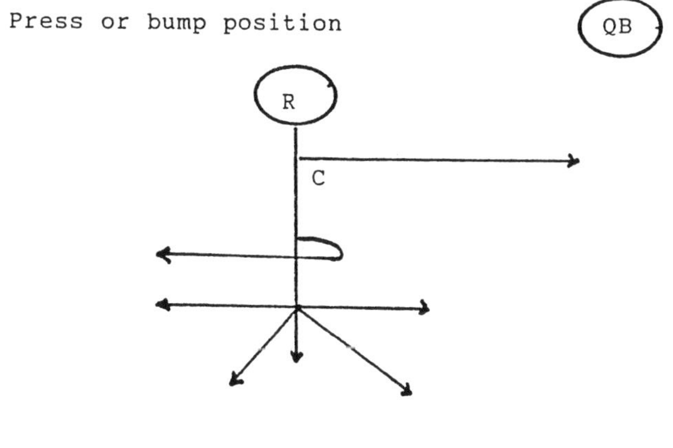

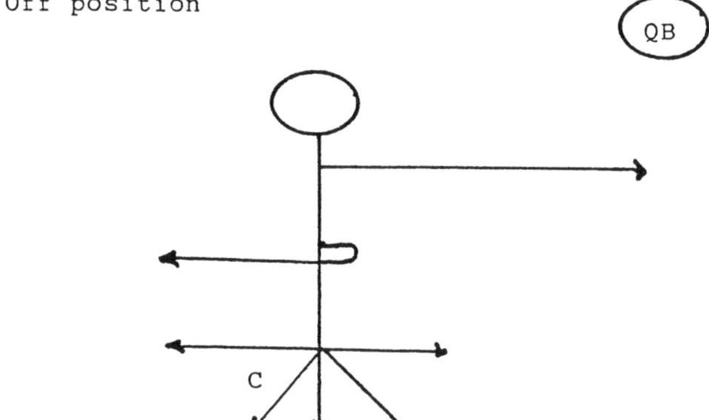

Note: Corners and free safeties should work from these positions against receivers who run all of the above routes.

GROUP DRILLS

Eagle Inside-Run Drill vs. Two Backs (Diagram 9 14)

The defensive personnel used in this drill are the tackles, nose, Mac, and strong safety. Offensively, the tackles, guards, center, quarterback, and two running backs are the personnel needed. The three run actions and

DIAGRAM 9–14
Eagle Inside-Run Drill vs. Two Backs

Strongside dive

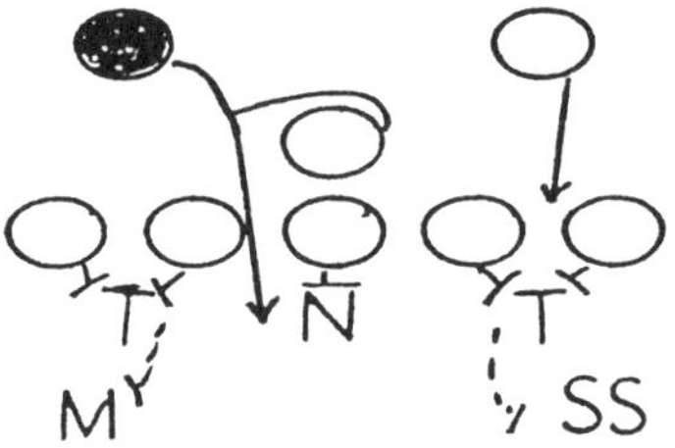

Fullback tackle trap strongside

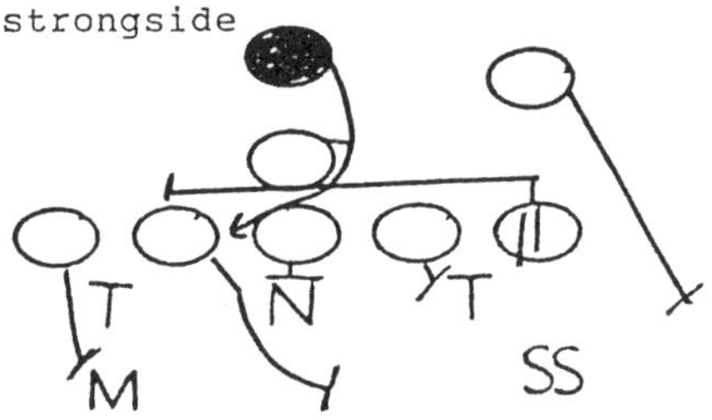

Strongside lead play

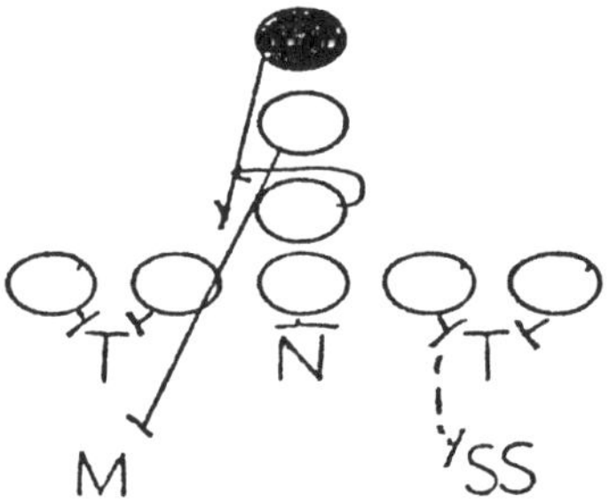

blocking schemes most frequently seen from two-back offensive sets are the dive, tackle trap, and lead plays. Although the defensive players know that the design of the drill permits only inside runs, it is a very effective way to get many repetitions of plays in a short period of time.

Eagle Inside-Run Drill vs. One Back
(Diagram 9–15)

The offensive and defensive personnel are the same as in the Eagle two-back drill, except the strong safety is not involved. The plays run are

DIAGRAM 9–15
Eagle Inside-Run Drill vs. One Back

Strongside fullback dive

Fullback trap strongside

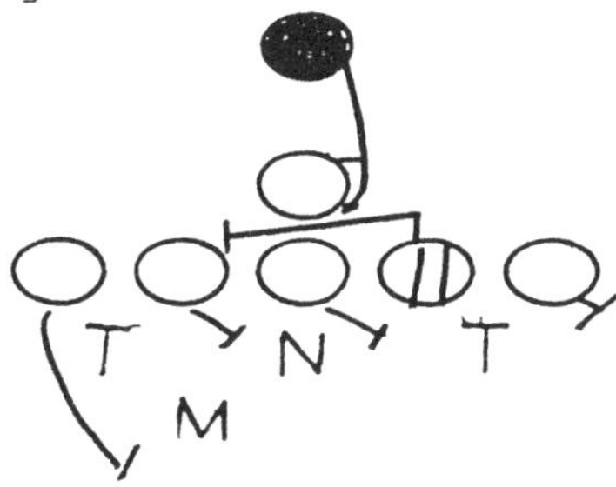

Note: Both of these plays can be run with the back in the halfback position. The dive with the back lined up strongside and the trap with the back weakside.

the strongside fullback dive, with the back behind the center or offset in the halfback position to the strong side. The fullback guard trap is the other play run, with the fullback lined up behind the center or offset in the halfback position to the weak side.

Hawk Inside-Run Drill vs. Two Backs (Diagram 9–16)

The same offensive and defensive personnel are used in the Hawk inside-run drills as are used in the Eagle inside-run drills. The plays run are the halfback dive, the halfback tackle trap, and the inside lead play to the strong side. These are the inside running plays that offensive teams will run most frequently against the Hawk type of alignment from two-back formations.

DIAGRAM 9–16
Hawk Inside-Run Drill vs. Two Backs

Halfback Dive

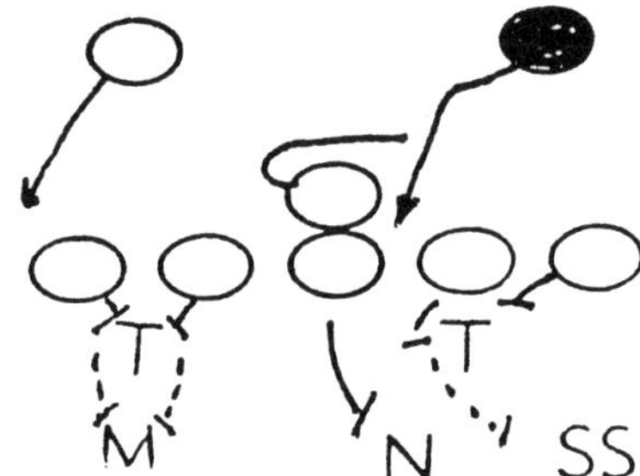

Halfback Tackle Trap

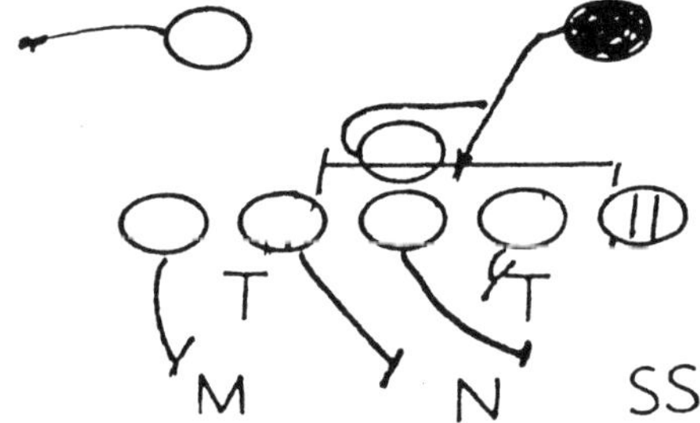

Tailback inside lead play strongside

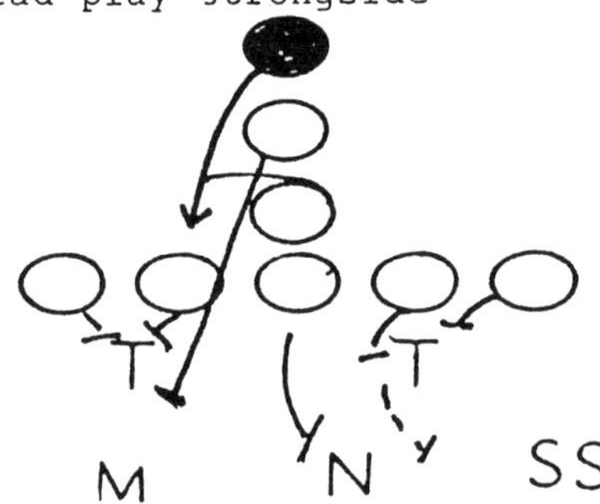

Hawk Inside-Run Drill vs. One Back (Diagram 9–17)

The personnel remain the same as above, except the strong safety does not participate in this drill. The fullback dive and tackle trap are the plays utilized in this drill. The back can be offset strongside for the dive and weakside for the trap.

DIAGRAM 9–17
Hawk Inside-Run Drill vs. One Back

Fullback Dive Strongside

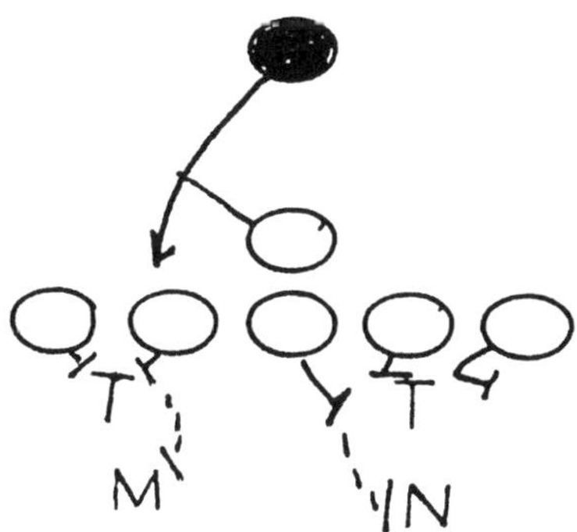

Fullback Tackle Trap Strongside

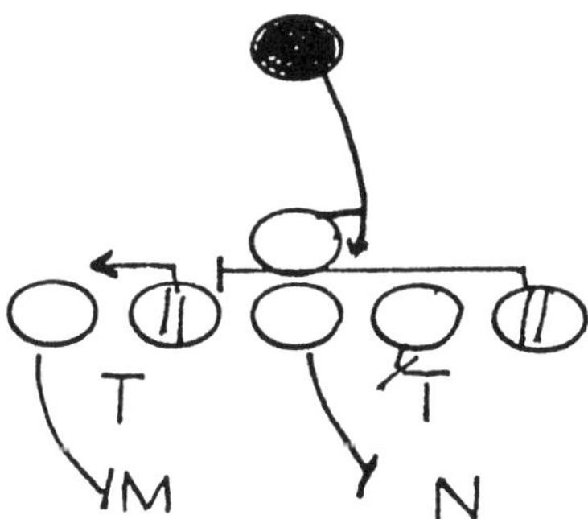

HALF-LINE DRILLS

Eagle Strongside-Run Drill vs. Two Backs (Diagram 9—18)

The defensive personnel in this drill are the outside linebacker, "B" linebacker, tackle, nose, and Mac; offensive personnel are the tight end,

DIAGRAM 9—18
Eagle Strongside-Run Drill vs. Two Backs

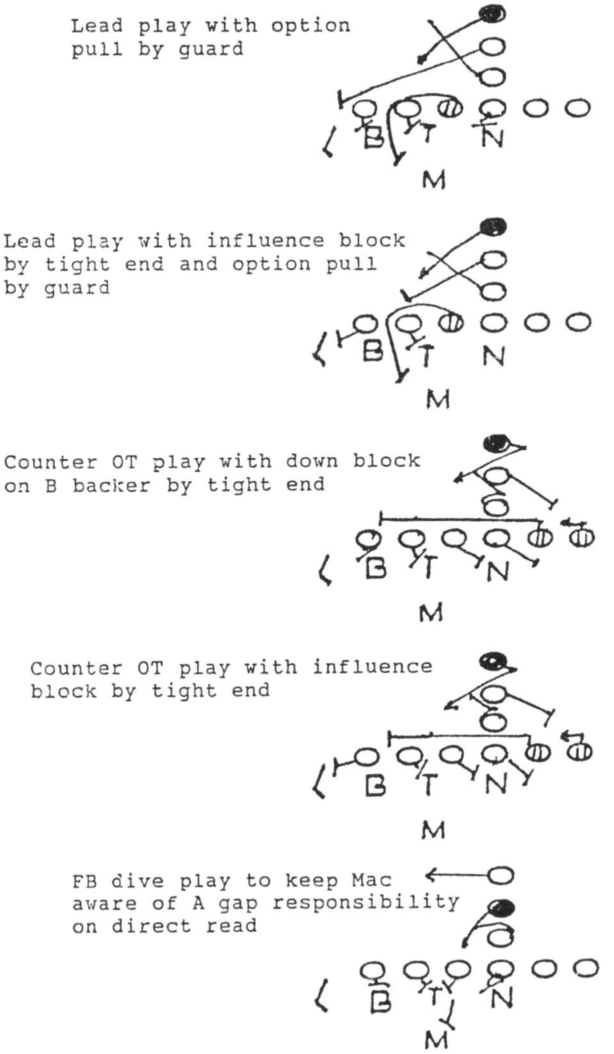

tackles, guards, center, quarterback, and two running backs. In this drill the nose will either two-gap the center or charge to the weakside "A" gap. The weakside guard and tackle are necessary in the drill in order to be able to run the strongside counter OT play. Although there are times when the "B" linebacker is lined up in an outside shade on the tight end, he should line up head up or slightly inside the tight end.

The lead play from the I formation or a strong formation is the most frequent play run to the strong side of the Eagle defense. The play can be run with several different blocking combinations. The variations of this play involve the fullback used as a lead blocker on either the outside linebacker, the "B" linebacker, or the Mac.

The counter OT play can be run two different ways. The most frequent is with a down block or a base block on the "B" backer by the tight end. However, some teams will influence or bluff the "B" linebacker with the tight end. When this happens, the tight end blocks out on the outside linebacker and the first puller blocks the "B" linebacker.

The fullback dive play is run in this drill for two basic reasons. One is to keep the defenders from overplaying the outside play and thus reducing the effectiveness of the drill. The other is to keep Mac aware of the "A" gap responsibility. When the ball attacks the strongside "A" gap, Mac must put the ball on his inside pad. He makes the tackle from the outside in, which means he makes the tackle with his inside shoulder. Since the strong safety in some adjustments must play over the tight end and is required to make the same plays the "B" linebacker does, it is wise to insert the strong safety in this drill in place of the "B" linebacker and allow him to work against these plays.

If the strongside drill is to be run utilizing one-back formations, the running plays used should be limited to the counter OT and fullback dive.

The same running plays can be run against the Hawk defense that are run against the Eagle. As with the Eagle, the counter OT and fullback dive are the only one-back plays that should be run.

Eagle Weakside or Open-Side Drill
(Diagram 9–19)

The defensive personnel in this drill are the outside linebacker, tackle, nose, and strong safety. The offensive personnel are the tackles, guards, center, quarterback, and two running backs.

The nose tackle in this drill must two-gap. He cannot be sent weakside as there are no plays that can be run to that side effectively if the nose slants to that side.

The keys to successfully defensing running plays to this side of the formation are that the tackle can never be reach-blocked by the guard, the strong safety must take all blockers with his inside pad, and the outside

DIAGRAM 9–19
Eagle Weakside or Open-Side Drill

```
Weakside toss or FB handoff HB
 lead on outside linebacker and
guard - Tackle combo block on
tackle
```

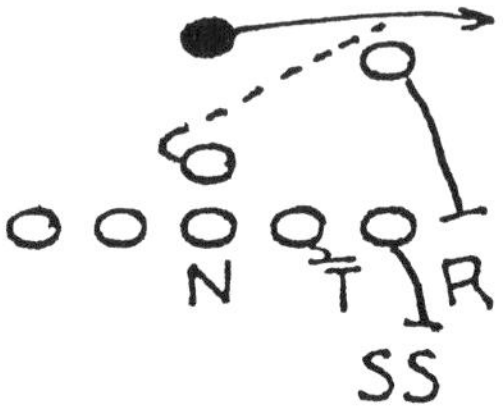

```
Same play as above but with option
pull by guard
```

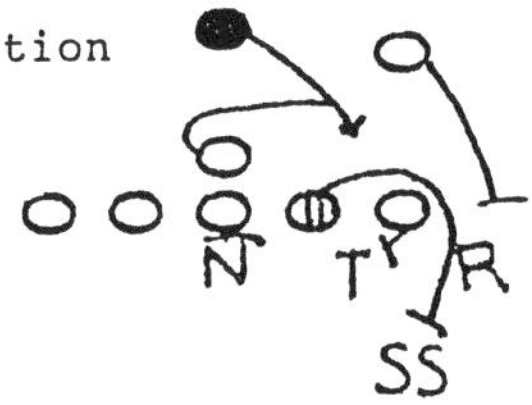

```
FB handoff with block out by tackle
on outside linebacker - reach block
on tackle by guard and lead block
on strong safety by HB
```

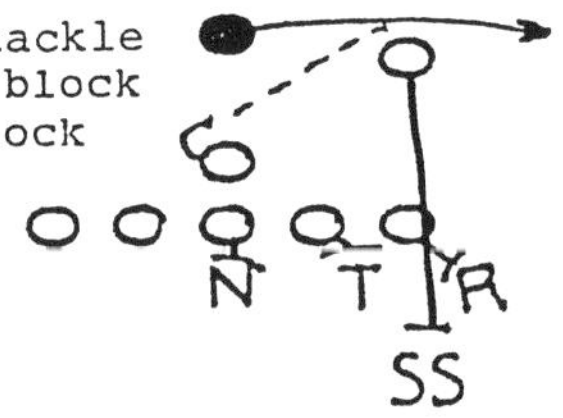

```
Counter OT play
```

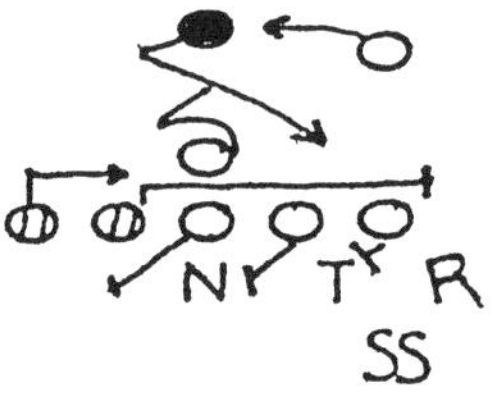

linebacker must force or keep the ball inside him but squeeze the cutback lane. It is really important that the strong safety take all blockers on with his inside pad so that if the outside linebacker does lose contain, the strong safety is able to serve as a secondary contain or force man. The "B" linebacker should be worked in the strong safety position at times since he plays in that position in open-formation adjustments. The running plays used in this drill are weakside handoffs or tosses to the fullback. These plays are base or man blocked, with various combinations of schemes used.

The counter OT play to the weak side is also a play that must be run in this drill. This is the reason the strongside guard and tackle must be included in this drill.

Under Skeleton Eagle and Hawk Defense (Diagram 9–20)

The defensive personnel in this drill consist of the "B" linebacker, Mac, nose linebacker, and strong safety. The nose linebacker must be there because he is involved as a pass defender in zone coverages. Offensively,

DIAGRAM 9–20
Under Skeleton Eagle and Hawk Defense

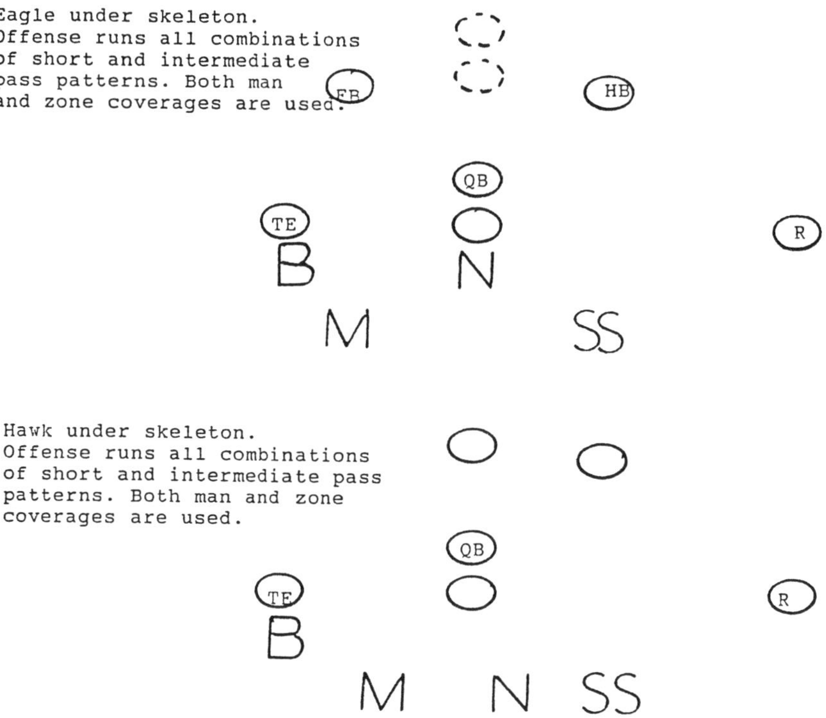

Note: This is an excellent way to work on zone and man coverages with the short defenders. This drill allows the short defenders repetitions on the pass routes they are responsible for. Also gives Mac and B backer and Mac and strong safety the opportunity to work on those situations where they play in and out coverage on two receivers.

the tight end, quarterback, and two running backs are required to run the drill.

The nose linebacker should stem on and off the line of scrimmage. In zone coverages, the nose should execute his responsibility from positions both on and off the line.

Equal amounts of zone and man-for-man pass coverages should be used. The offense should use all combinations of pass routes involving tight ends and running backs.

This drill is an excellent way to teach man-for-man base techniques as well as any combination coverage adjustments. It is also an excellent way to teach zone pattern reads as they relate to flare controls by the offense.

Although one-on-one and man-for-man coverage drills are effective teaching tools, I like this drill much better because more people get more repetitions in the same amount of time. When one-on-one drills are going on, two people are working and everyone else is watching.

Hollow (Deep) Skeleton vs. Corners and Free Safety (Diagram 9–21)

The defensive personnel in this drill are the corners and free safety. The offensive players needed to run the drill are the receivers, tight ends, and quarterback.

Three-deep zone is the only type of pass coverage used in this drill. Deep patterns such as go routes, seams, corners, and posts, as well as deep sideline cuts are the only ones that should be run. Four receivers running go routes on the same play should also be used. The four verticals up the field teach the three deep defenders how to play this particular pass play.

The emphasis defensively should be on reading the deep patterns, seeing and reading the quarterback, and playing the ball in the air.

The theory behind this drill is that zone pass defense teams do not get enough balls thrown up the field against them in practice. Most of the time, offensive teams drop the ball off underneath against zone coverages. As a result, the deep defenders never get enough opportunities to defend against deep balls in practice. This drill creates opportunities for this to happen.

Run Drill (9 on 8) (Diagram 9–22)

The defensive personnel in the run drill are all of the defensive players except the corners and free safety. Offensively, all players except the wide receivers are used.

DIAGRAM 9–21
Hollow (Deep) Skeleton vs. Corners and Free Safety

Three-deep zone defenses are used in this drill - only
combinations of deep routes are run. A tight end or running
back are added to the drill as a #2 receiver weak side in
order to run pass patterns that involve four receivers up
the field in order to stretch the three-deep coverage.

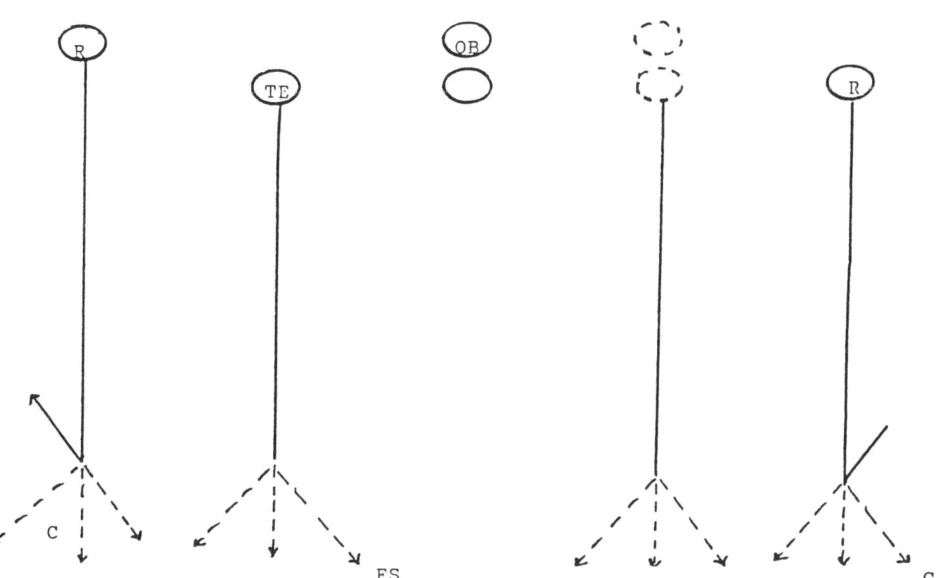

Note: Strong safety may be substituted for free safety
in this drill since some adjustments cause him to be a deep
middle defender. Also free safety should take some turns at
corner in this drill since some adjustments require him to be
a deep outside 1/3 defender.

All inside and perimeter runs are used in this drill. An occasional
play-action pass should be added to increase the value of the drill from a
key and reaction standpoint. This drill should be similar to a scrimmage
but with no tackling. This drill teaches technique and gap responsibilities
against specific plays.

It is important that the defensive tackle away from the direction of

DIAGRAM 9–22
Run Drill (9 on 8)

Run drill hawk and Eagle vs. two backs.
All two-back runs from all two-back offensive formations.

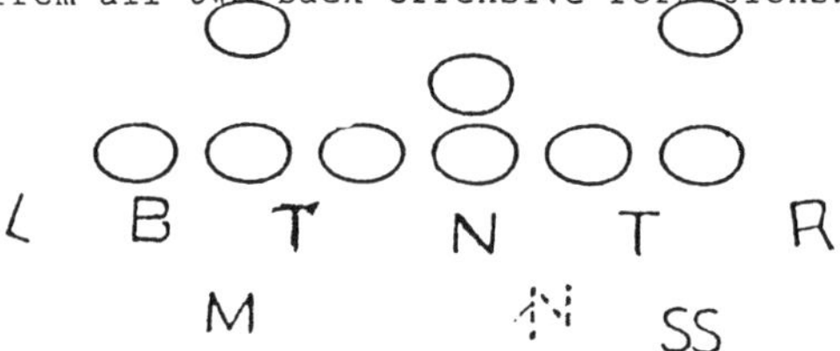

Run drill hawk and Eagle vs. one back.
Balanced offensive set.
All one-back runs from balanced one-back formation. Counter OT
play weak and strong should be high frequency plays along with FB
dive in A gap weak and strong.

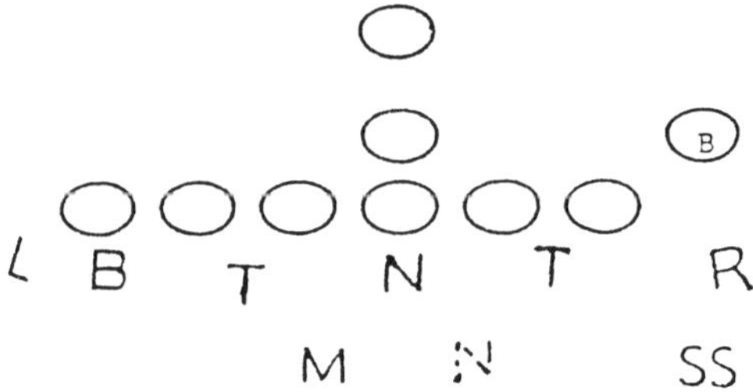

Run drill hawk and Eagle vs. one back.
Trips offensive set. Weakside counter OT and FB dive in A gap
weak and strong should be the plays run most frequently.

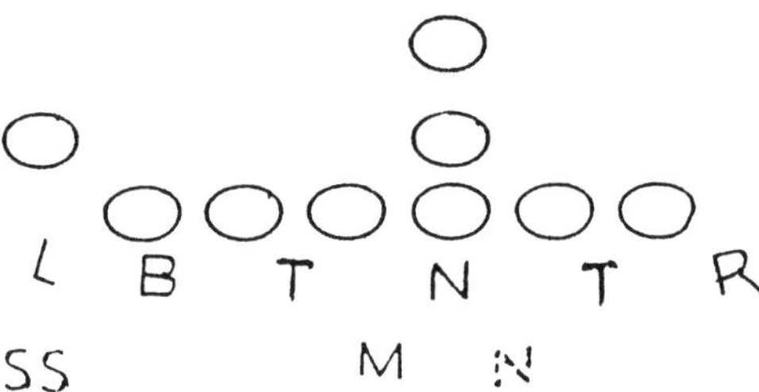

the play slow down his charge when plays are run away from him. If he does not, he will disrupt plays run away from him.

In this drill both the Eagle and Hawk defenses should be used. All combinations of both two-back and one-back sets should be used along with all combinations of one, two, and three tight ends.

Pass Skeleton vs. Multiple Formations (Diagram 9–23)

The defensive personnel involved are all the defensive players, except the outside linebacker and the tackles. Offensively, the two wide receivers, two running backs, a tight end, center, and quarterback. There should also be an additional tight end and wide receiver available in order to work against the various one-back multiple-tight-end and one-back three-wide-receiver formations. All drop-back routes should be thrown.

The nose linebacker should drop from the line of scrimmage or from his dropped-off Hawk position.

In order to ensure proper pass releases by the tight ends and running back, 30-gallon garbage cans should be used on the line of scrimmage in the areas normally occupied by the offensive tackles.

TEAM DRILLS

Team drills in practice should be divided into categories by down and distance. First down and second down and five yards or less should consist of working against running plays, play-action passes, and screen passes.

The plays selected to work against situations such as second down and long (seven or more years to go) should consist of drop-back passes, draw plays, screen passes, and any other play used in these situations.

There are a couple of areas that need to be addressed in team work using the Eagle defense. One is the concern for the high number of high-velocity collisions between the outside linebackers (R and L) and the blockers who are assigned to blocking them. Since the defensive design requires these players to attack with high velocity, the number of outside runs with pullers or running backs blocking the perimeter must be monitored. Also, the problem of cutoff block on the tackles on plays run away from them has to be addressed. One of the most effective ways to block the tackles on plays run away from them is to cut-block or low-block them. It makes very little sense to use this type of block against your own

DIAGRAM 9–23
Pass Skeleton vs. Multiple Formations

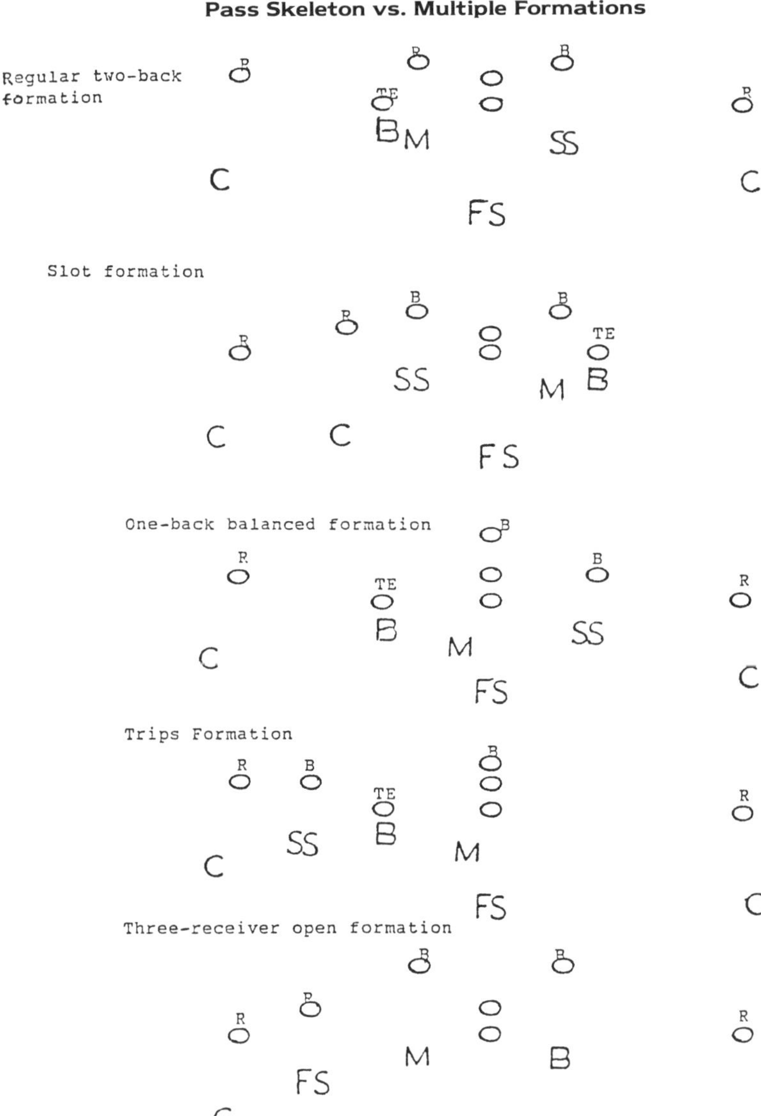

players because of the high risk of injuries. As a result, it is best to slow down the tackle away from the play in order to let the play develop so that the players on the side that the play is run to will get ample work on these actions.

10

Pass Coverage, Dogs, and Blitzes

The Eagle and Hawk alignments place eight players in a good position to rush the passer. All players, except the corners and the free safety, line up close enough to the passer to be effective rushers. In other words, this defense, by the nature of the placement of players, lends itself to effective dogging or blitzing by several players.

This defensive scheme is best suited to playing man-for-man pass coverages. By utilizing man-for-man schemes, five players can be committed to rushing the passer and yet be able to play with a free safety.

This alignment does not lend itself to the utilization of zone coverages like balanced seven-man-front defenses do. However, because five linebackers are used in the scheme, with one of them a nose linebacker on or off the line of scrimmage, this eight-man front makes it possible to play effective zone coverage.

In addition to dogs and blitzes the three basic coverages used in the Eagle and Hawk defenses are man-for-man with a free safety, three-deep zone, and two-deep zone.

EAGLE AND HAWK BASE PASS COVERAGES

Eagle and Hawk Man Coverage
(Diagram 10—1)

The outside linebackers, tackles, and nose linebacker are all pass rushers. Mac gives the nose a call on every down. The nose may rush the

DIAGRAM 10–1
Eagle and Hawk Man Coverage

Two-Back Formations

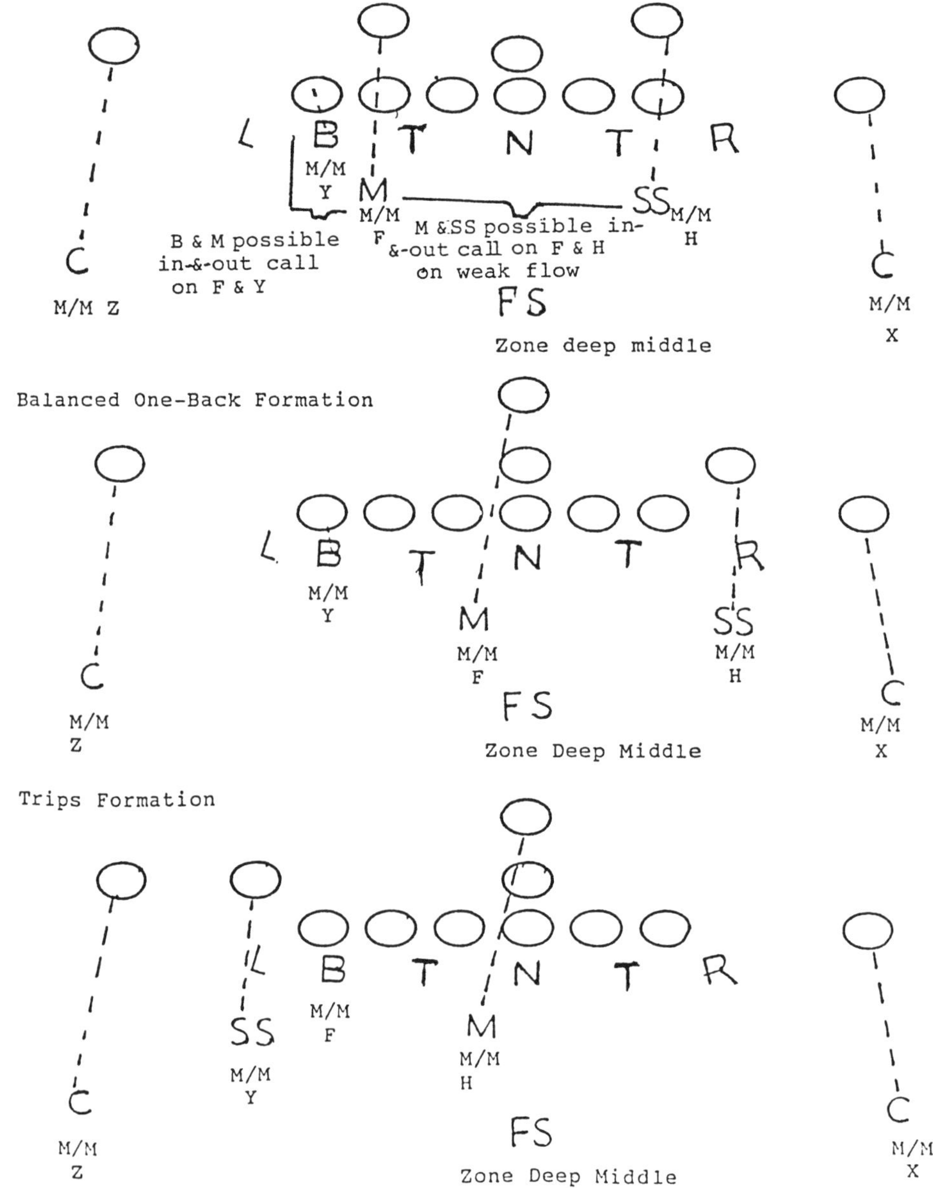

Balanced One-Back Formation

Trips Formation

"A" gap to the side of the call or he can run a game with the tackle to the side of the call. He also has the option of running a game with both the tackle and the outside linebacker to that side.

Run force. The outside linebackers (R and L) are the force men on both sides of the formation. However, on the open side of the offensive formation the linebacker may bounce the ball outside to the strong safety, who is a secondary force man.

"B" linebacker. The "B" linebacker is responsible for covering the tight end man-for-man. He aligns either head up on or slightly inside the tight end when he is not involved in a combination coverage with the Mac linebacker. When there is a back lined up in the halfback position on the strong side, the "B" linebacker is involved with in-and-out coverage with the Mac on the tight end and near back. When the "B" linebacker is involved with in-and-out coverage just before the snap, he lines up in a slight outside shade on the tight end. With an in-and-out call, the "B" linebacker's coverage is determined by the release of the tight end. If the tight end releases inside, he covers the back in all situations, except if both backs go to the weak side. If this happens, the "B" linebacker covers the tight end even though he released inside. If the tight end releases outside, he covers him in all situations. If the "B" linebacker's coverage blocks, he should go to him and physically engage him with his hands to protect against his man catching a screen pass. The technique used by the "B" linebacker on the tight end should be an inside-out jam trail technique. If he is covering a back out of the backfield, he should use an inside-out catch technique. This means he should always have an inside position on the back and not let him release inside on any pass routes.

Mac linebacker. The Mac linebacker is responsible for covering the back to the tight-end side of the formation in two-back offensive sets. When he makes an in-and-out call with the "B" linebacker, he will cover either the tight end or the back to his side, depending on the action. With an in-and-out call, if the tight end releases inside the "B" linebacker and the strong back releases or blocks to the strong side, the Mac covers the tight end. If both backs release to the weak side, Mac plays in-and-out coverage on the two backs with the strong safety. If both backs release to the strong side of the formation, Mac plays in-and-out coverage on the backs with the "B" linebacker if the tight end releases inside. If the tight end releases outside with both backs strong, Mac has in-and-out coverage on the backs with the strong safety. In a one-back formation the Mac linebacker is responsible for the back in the backfield. The Mac uses an inside-out catch-trail technique, never allowing the man he is covering to get inside him.

Strong safety.   The strong safety is responsible for man-for-man coverage on the number-two receiver to the weak side of the formation in all formations except trips. In a trips formation he is responsible for the number-two receiver to the strong side. The strong safety plays in-and-out coverage on the backs with Mac if both backs release to the weak side of the formation in two-back sets. With both backs strong and an inside release by the tight end, he covers the tight end. If both backs release to the strong side and the tight end releases outside, he plays in and out on the backs with Mac. If there are three wide receivers in the game, the strong safety is a deep middle one-third defender. When he is covering a back out of the backfield, he uses the same inside-out catch technique that is used by Mac. When he is covering a tight end in a one-back set, he uses the same inside-out trail technique that is used by the "B" linebacker when he is covering a tight end.

Corners.   The corners are responsible for man-for-man coverage on the wide receivers wherever they line up.

If the offense lines up in a slot formation, the weak corner goes across the formation and covers the slot or the number-two receiver to the strong side. This is a match-up defense, which means it is very important that the corners are always lined up over and covering the wide receivers.

Free safety.   The free safety is a deep middle one-third defender against most offensive formations. However, when there are three wide receivers in the game, the free safety is responsible for the third wide receiver man-for-man. The strong safety becomes the deep middle one-third defender. This adjustment is made to ensure the best possible coverage match-ups since the free safety is usually, by athletic ability and speed, better equipped to cover a wide receiver man-for-man.

Eagle and Hawk Zone Coverage
(Diagram 10–2)

The outside linebackers and the tackles are pass rushers. The nose is a pass defender in all coverages. He is an open-side or weakside hook defender versus all formations except trips. Against the trips formation, the nose is a curl-to-flat defender to the weak side. As a variation of zone coverage versus trips, a change call may be made. With a change call the nose becomes a pass rusher and the weakside outside linebacker is the curl-to-flat defender. When Eagle zone is called, the Mac gives the nose a right or left call, sending him to his pass coverage side. On the snap, the nose makes his move to the side of his pass coverage. If pass shows, he

DIAGRAM 10–2
Eagle and Hawk Zone Coverage

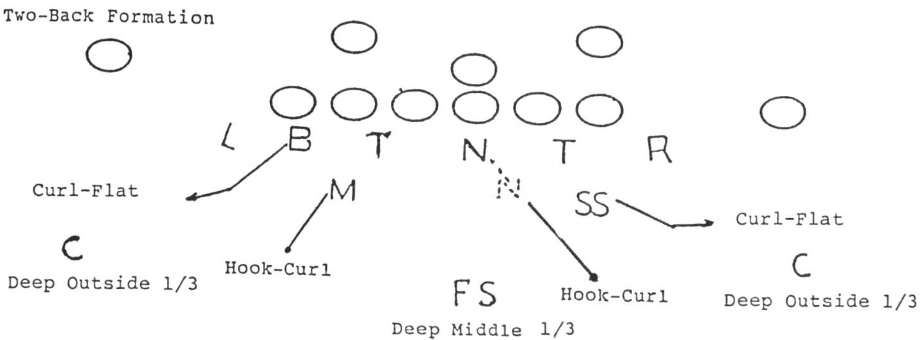

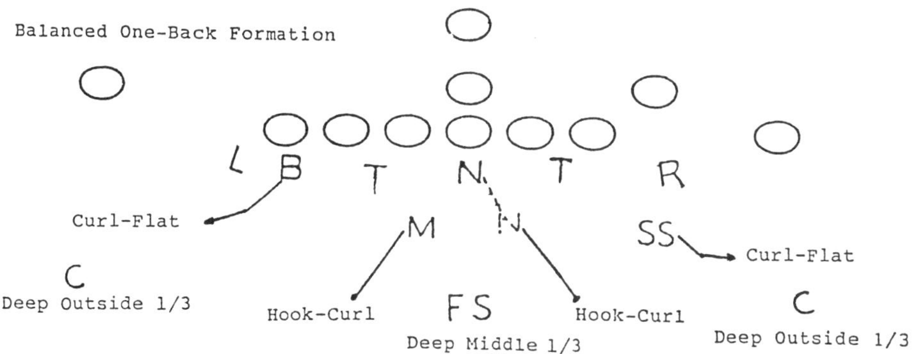

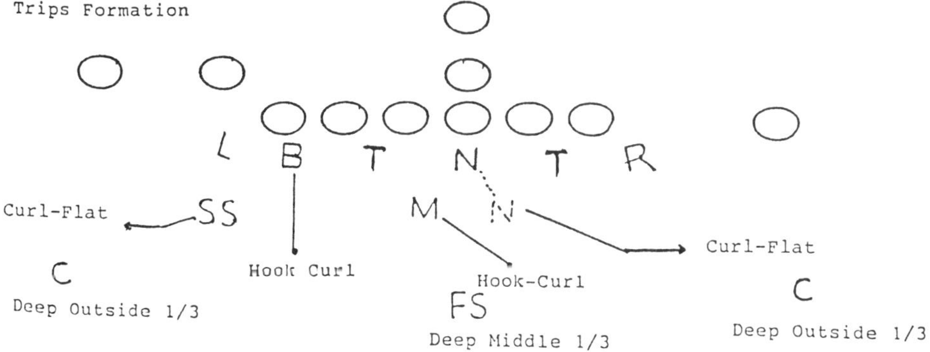

drops to his pass zone responsibility. If a run play develops, the nose plays his normal run gap responsibility.

Run force. The outside linebackers are responsible for run force to their side. However, if the adjustment of the strong safety places his alignment outside the R or L, he makes a sky force call and becomes the force man to that side.

"B" linebacker. The "B" linebacker is either a curl-to-flat defender or a hook-to-curl defender, depending on the direction of the rotation of the secondary. If the rotation is to the side of the "B" linebacker, he is a hook-to-curl defender. If the rotation is away from him, the "B" linebacker is a curl-to-flat defender. If an open-formation adjustment is made, the "B" linebacker is a curl-to-flat defender on the weak side since the rotation will be away from him or to the strong side.

Mac linebacker. Mac is a tight-end-side or strongside hook-to-curl defender versus most formations. However, when a trips formation adjustment is made, Mac is an open-side or weakside hook defender.

Nose linebacker. The nose linebacker is a hook-to-curl defender to the weak side or open side of the formations. However, versus trips he is a curl-to-flat defender to the weak side unless a change call is made. With a change call, the nose becomes a pass rusher and the outside linebacker on his side becomes the weak curl-to-flat defender. In the Eagle defense, the nose lines up on the line of scrimmage, starts to his normal run gap responsibility, and when he reads pass drops to his pass coverage responsibility. In the Hawk defense, he stems to his normal position and executes his responsibilities. If Eagle zone is played against a trips formation, the nose should stem to his Hawk alignment and execute his zone drop from that position. The Hawk alignment places him in a better position to drop to his curl-to-flat responsibility.

Strong safety. The strong safety is a curl-to-flat defender on the weak side of all defensive formations except trips. If the offensive team lines up in trips, he is a curl-to-flat defender on the strong side. If the offensive team motions to a trips formation, the safeties roll and the strong safety rotates to the free-safety position or the deep middle. If the strong safety's alignment against a trips or double position places him outside the outside linebacker, he must make a sky force call and contain all runs to his side.

Corners. The corners are responsible for the deep outside one-third zones to their side versus all formations except the two-back slot formation. Both corners line up to the strong side of a slot formation. The outside corner is a deep outside one-third defender; the inside corner is a deep middle defender. If the offensive team motions from a slot to a regular formation, the inside corner moves across the formation with the motion man and becomes a deep outside one-third defender.

Free safety. The free safety is a deep middle one-third defender. If the offensive team goes to a trips formation by motion, the free safety rotates to the trips side and becomes a curl-to-flat defender to the strong side. Versus a three-wide-receiver formation, he lines up over the third wide receiver and plays his appropriate zone responsibility.

TWO-DEEP ZONE

Eagle and Hawk Two-Deep Zone (Diagram 10—3)

The outside linebackers and tackles are pass rushers. The Mac gives the nose linebacker a right or left call on every down. This establishes the direction of the line charge of the nose as well as the direction of his pass drop.

Run force. The corners are responsible for run force on their respective sides. Because they have force outside them, the outside linebackers are able to rush at a much tighter angle than they do in man coverages or zone with no force man outside them.

"B" linebacker. The "B" linebacker has man-for-man coverage on the tight end or the number-two receiver on the strong side of the formation. He should use a head up or slight inside alignment on the man he is covering. He should use an inside trail technique and never allow the receiver to run an inside or crossing route. It is very important that the "B" linebacker use his hands and jam the man he is covering on the line.

Mac linebacker. The Mac is a hook-to-curl defender strongside. Since the tight end is the man-for-man coverage responsibility of the "B" linebackers, he is taken out of the pattern read. Therefore, Mac reads patterns like he is on the weak side of the formation. That is, he reads the back as the number two in the formation and gets his lateral stretch from the release of the back as he reads the quarterback. Mac has the responsibility of avoiding any collisions with the tight end and the "B" backer who covers him.

Nose linebacker. The nose linebacker is a hook-to-curl defender to the weak side of the formation. His drop and pattern reads are the same as they are in Eagle or Hawk zone except that he must be ready to carry the number-two receiver on his side deeper than he does in a three-deep zone. In a three-deep zone he carries the number-two receiver to his side 10 to 12 yards deep, but in the two-deep zone coverage he must carry him 12 to 15 yards deep. The reason for this is that the two safeties cannot be stretched by two upfield receivers on one side of the formation. With the nose carrying or covering the vertical release of the number-two receiver,

DIAGRAM 10–3
Eagle and Hawk Two-Deep Zone

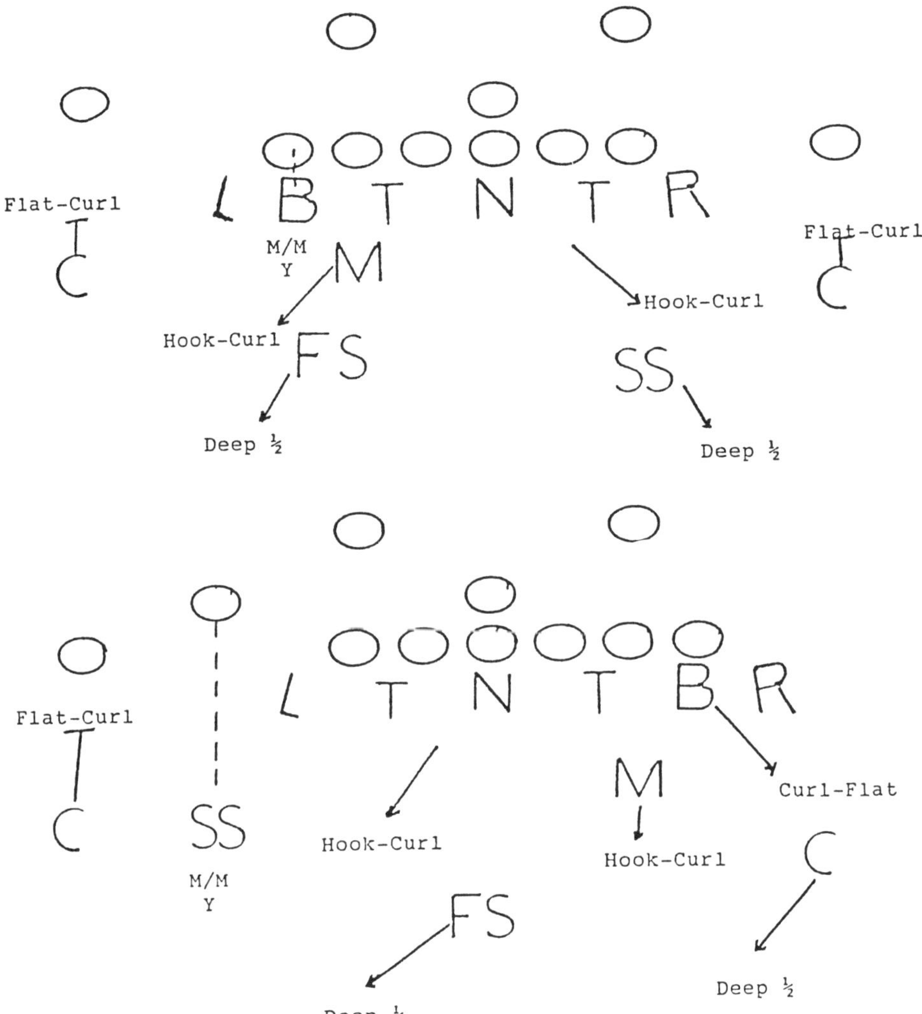

he will force the quarterback to elevate any upfield throw, thus giving the safety time to react and make a play on the thrown ball.

Strong safety. The strong safety is the weakside deep half defender. Just before the snap he should stem or deepen his alignment to 12 to 15 yards from the line of scrimmage, approximately two yards inside the number on a standard NFL field. He must get depth quickly as he reads passing plays. He is responsible for all deep patterns thrown to the weakside half of the field. Depth is important because the more depth he has, the more his range or ability to make plays on deep throws will be increased.

Free safety. The free safety is the strongside deep half defender. Just before the snap he should stem his alignment from the middle one-third to the strongside half of the field, approximately two yards from the numbers, 12 to 15 yards deep. He must get depth quickly as he reads passing plays. He is responsible for all deep patterns thrown to the strongside half of the field. Again, depth is very important in determining the range or amount of area the safeties are able to cover.

Corners. The corners align head up on X and Z from the off position, seven yards deep, or stem to a press position. On the snap they must jam the receiver and force his flat release. The corners must read the pass release of the number-two receiver on their side of the formation. If the number-two receiver releases upfield and continues deep, the corner must cover the X or the Z on all upfield routes. If the number-two receiver runs a route in the flat, the corner must cover him. If the number-two receiver blocks or goes away, the corner must begin to drop and carry number one but look for crossing receivers. If a crosser does appear, the corner must cover him. Generally, depending on the pattern read, the coverage responsibility of the corner is described as the outside zone extending from the line of scrimmage to the goal line. The corner is responsible for force or contain on all outside runs.

DOGS

One of the advantages of the Eagle and Hawk defenses is that they place eight players in excellent positions to rush the passer. The "B" linebacker, the Mac linebacker, and the strong safety are all lined up either on the line of scrimmage or within four yards of it. This means they are in good positions to dog or blitz and to be effective in rushing the quarter-back. In addition, the dogging system involving these players is simplified by the fact that the free safety is available to assume the coverage responsibility of any player who is the one involved in the dog. Essentially this system of dogging is an offshoot of the man coverage used in this defense. In other words, the dogs are Eagle or Hawk man coverage with no free safety in the middle.

"B" Linebacker Dog
(Diagram 10–4)

Outside linebacker.   The R and L are hard outside contain pass rushers. They are the force men on all runs.

"B" linebacker.   The "B" linebacker, from his position over the tight end, blitzes through the "C" gap. He can make an "A" call, which tells the tackle on his side to work outside through the offensive tackle and indicates that the "B" linebacker will take a step toward the tight end and then blitz through the strongside "A" gap. The step toward the tight end is essential because it allows time for the defensive tackle to lean or open up the inside gap for the "B" linebacker to blitz in—against a two-back open formation, the "B" linebacker will blitz the weakside "A" gap from his alignment on the weak side of the formation.

Weak tackle.   The weak tackle executes his normal Eagle charge low and hard for penetration in the weak "B" gap.

Strong tackle.   The strong tackle executes his normal hard "B" gap charge working for penetration. It is important that the tackle make an inside pass rush move on the guard if he pass blocks him. If the "B" linebacker makes an "A" call, the strongside tackle charges hard through the inside shoulder of the offensive tackle.

Nose.   The Mac linebacker gives the nose a right or left call in the direction away from the "B" linebacker. He charges low and hard into the "A" gap away from the "B" linebacker. The nose may run a game with the weak tackle once the direction of his charge is established.

Mac.   Mac plays his normal man coverage, which is man-for-man on the back to his side of the formation. Mac has the possibility of playing in-and-out coverage on F and H with the strong safety against two-back formations. Versus one-back sets, Mac covers the remaining back man-for-man. If the back offsets to the weak side, Mac must adjust his alignment to place himself in a position to cover him.

Strong safety.   The strong safety plays his normal man responsibility, which is man-for-man coverage on the number-two receiver to the weak side of the formation in all formations except trips. Versus trips, he is responsible for the number-two receiver to the strong side of the forma-tion. The strong safety has the possibility of playing in-and-out coverage on the F and H with the Mac linebacker when both backs release to either the strong side or the weak side of the formation.

Corners.   The corners have man-for-man coverage on the X and Z. Against a slot formation they have man-for-man coverage on the number-one and number-two receivers to the strong side.

DIAGRAM 10–4
"B" Linebacker Dog

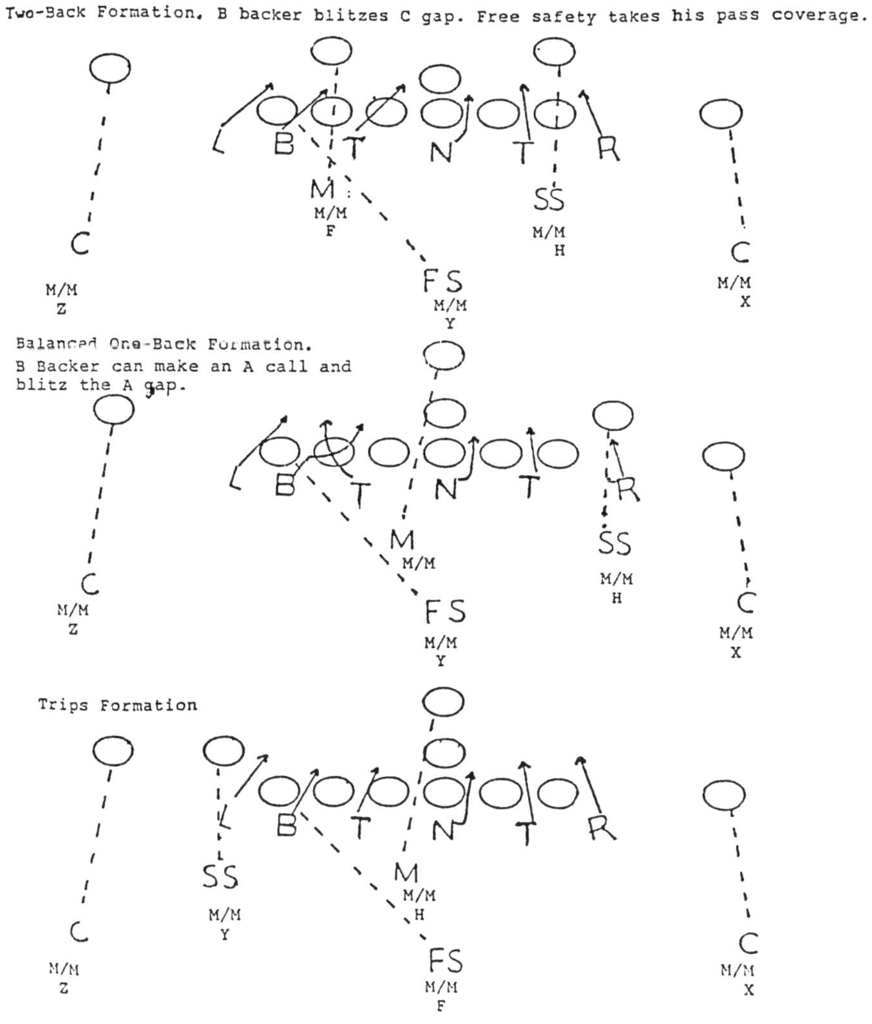

Two-Back Formation. B backer blitzes C gap. Free safety takes his pass coverage.

Balanced One-Back Formation.
B Backer can make an A call and
blitz the A gap.

Trips Formation

Free safety. The free safety replaces the "B" linebacker in coverage, which means that he has man-for-man coverage on the number-two receiver to the strong side of the formation. In most regular two-back and slot formations this would be the tight end. Against a two-back open formation, the free safety is responsible for the H or the number-two receiver to the weak side.

Eagle and Hawk Mac Dog
(Diagram 10–5)

Outside linebackers.   The R and L are hard outside contain pass rushers. They are the force men on all runs.

"B" linebacker.   The "B" linebacker has man-for-man coverage on the tight end. He has the possibility of having in-and-out coverage on the tight end and fullback with the free safety. This type of in-and-out coverage is usually desirable whenever there is a back lined up in the halfback position to the strong side.

Weak tackle.   The weak tackle takes his normal charge low and hard through the "B" gap, working for penetration. If Hawk Mac Dog is called, the weak tackle charges in a straight upfield charge rather than his slightly turned-in charge.

Strong tackle.   The strong tackle rushes low and hard through the "B" gap. It is important that he charge in more of a straight upfield charge. This type of charge prevents the offensive tackle from pushing or collapsing the tackle into the "A" gap with a down block. If the Mac gives the strong tackle a "B" call, this means the Mac is dogging through the "B" gap. With this call the strong tackle should charge hard through the strong "A" gap.

Mac.   Mac must give a right or left call to the nose. He should send the nose to the weakside "A" gap. The nose may run a game with the weak tackle. Mac can dog in two different gaps. If he does not make any call, Mac dogs through the strongside "A" gap. If Mac makes a "B" call, that tells the strong tackle to charge through the "A" gap with the Mac dogging through the strongside "B" gap. If Hawk Mac Dog is called, Mac charges through the strongside "A" gap. Also, in Hawk, Mac may make a cross call with the nose linebacker. If a cross call is made, the Mac and nose dog through the "A" gap to the opposite side. Mac indicates to the nose which of them will go first.

Nose.   The nose will get a right or left call indicating that his responsibility will be to charge through the weakside "A" gap. He may run a game with the weak tackle. If Hawk Mac Dog is called, the nose dogs through the weakside "A" gap. If Mac makes a cross call, the nose dogs through the strongside "A" gap. Mac will indicate which player is to go first in the cross call.

Strong safety.   The strong safety has man-for-man coverage on the H or the number-two receiver to the weak side of the formation in all formations except trips. Versus trips, the strong safety is man-for-man on the number-two receiver to the strong side of the formation.

DIAGRAM 10–5
Eagle and Hawk Mac Dog

Two-Back Formation. Mac blitzes A gap strongside. Free safety takes his pass coverage.

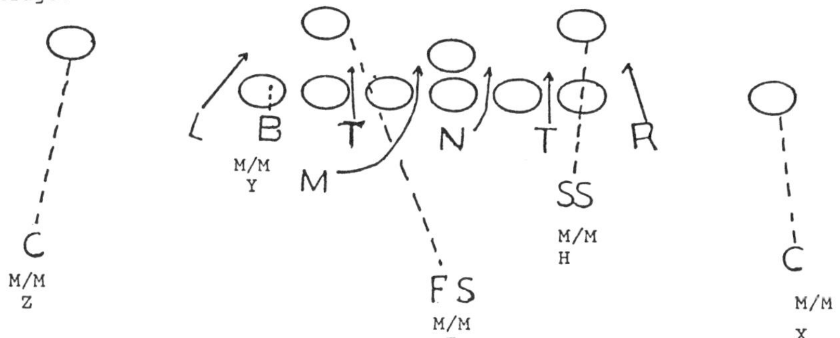

Hawk Mac Dog. Mac blitzes A gap strongside and nose blitzes A gap weakside.

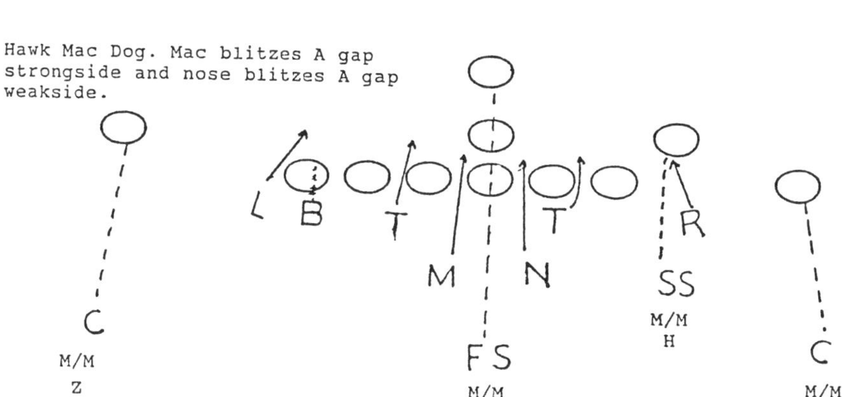

Hawk Mac Dog. Mac can make cross call. He and nose cross and blitz opposite A gaps, Mac calls who goes first.

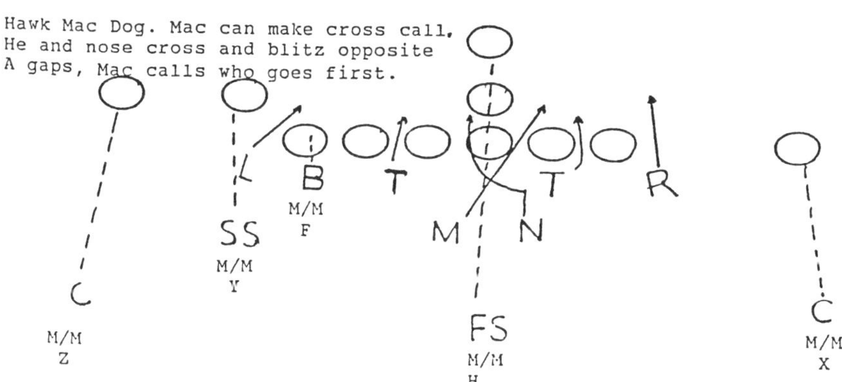

Corners.   The corners are responsible for man-for-man coverage on the wide receivers, the X and Z. In a slot formation they are responsible for the two receivers to the strong side.

Free safety.   The free safety replaces the Mac in coverage. He has man-for-man coverage on the fullback in regular two-back formation. When there is a back in the strong halfback position, he can make an in-and-out call to the "B" linebacker. The in-and-out call indicates that the free safety and "B" linebacker will play in-and-out coverage on the tight end and strong back, based on the releases of the two offensive players.

Eagle Safety Dog (Diagram 10–6)

Outside linebackers.   The R and L are hard outside contain pass rushers. They are the force men on all runs.

"B" linebacker.   The "B" linebacker has man-for-man coverage responsibility on the tight end. He also has the same in-and-out coverage possibilities with the Mac linebacker that he has in man coverage.

Strong tackle.   The strong tackle executes his normal Eagle charge low and hard for penetration in the weak "B" gap.

Weak tackle.   The weak tackle executes his normal hard "B" gap charge working for penetration. However, since the strong safety is dogging through the weak "A" gap, his charge should be more of a straight upfield as opposed to a pointed-in charge. This enables him to fight the pressure of a down block by the tackle better and thus prevents him from being collapsed down into the "A" gap where the strong safety is blitzing.

Nose.   The Mac linebacker gives the nose a right or left call sending him to the tight-end side or away from the strong safety. The nose charges low and hard through the strongside "A" gap. The nose has the option of running a game with the strongside tackle.

Mac linebacker.   The Mac linebacker is responsible for man-for-man coverage on the strong back. He also has the same in-and-out coverage responsibilities with the "B" linebacker that he has in man coverage. Versus one-back sets, Mac has man-for-man coverage on the remaining back.

Strong safety.   The strong safety dogs through the weakside "A" gap against all two-back formations. If the offensive team uses a one-back set, the strong safety covers the number-two receiver to the weak side in a balanced set and the number-two receiver to the strong side in a trips set. With one-back formations, the free safety replaces the strong safety and blitzes the weakside "A" gap.

DIAGRAM 10–6
Eagle Safety Dog

Two-Back Formation.
Strong Safety blitzes a gap weakside - Free Safety
covers H man/man.

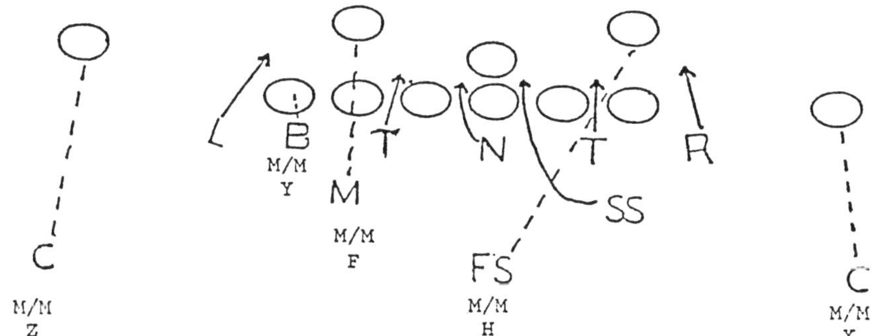

Balance one-back formation.
Free Safety blitzes A gap weakside
and Strong Safety covers H man/man.

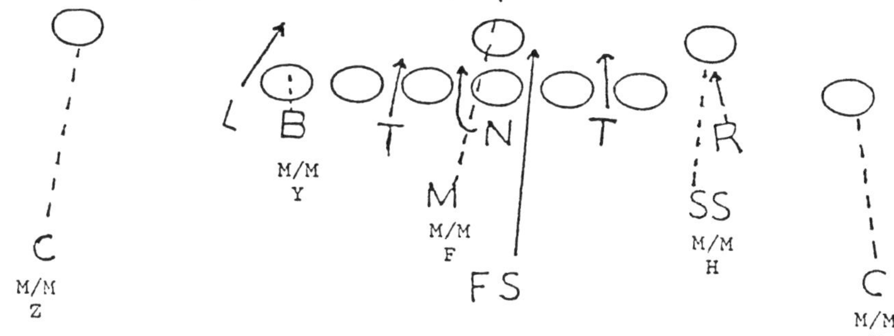

Trips formation.
Free Safety blitzes A gap weakside
and Strong Safety covers Y man/man.

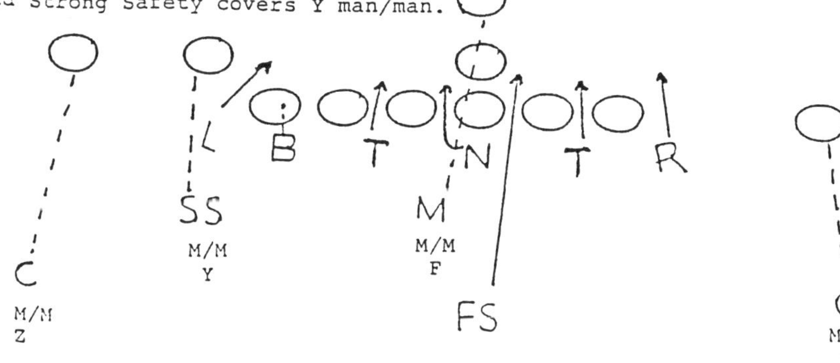

Corners.   The corners have the same coverage on the X and Z that they have in man coverage and in all the Eagle dogs.

Free safety.   The free safety has man-for-man coverage on the H or the number-two receiver to the weak side of the formation against all two-back formations. Against one-back formations, he replaces the strong safety and dogs through the weakside "A" gap. The "B" linebacker, the Mac, and the strong safety dogs are simple but effective ways to pressure the passing or running attacks of an offensive team. The fact that one man, the free safety, makes almost all the adjustments from a coverage standpoint really makes this a relatively simple system, which minimizes the chance for error.

BLITZES

Blitzing in the Eagle defense is facilitated by the fact that eight defensive players are lined up within five yards of the line of scrimmage. Since eight players are involved in the blitz, it is necessary for one or more of the blitzing players to have pass coverage responsibility if the offensive team releases all five of their eligible pass receivers. This responsibility, which is called blitz and peel, is given to the outside linebackers, or the R or L. Blitz and peel means that the outside linebacker has free contain blitz or rush unless his pass coverage responsibility releases his way. If this happens, he must cover the back man-for-man. If the back he is responsible for attempts to release through the line of scrimmage, the R or L becomes a free pass rusher. The linemen and blitzers have the responsibility for preventing a back releasing into the line from getting downfield by pinning or jamming him into the line of scrimmage.

Eagle Strong Blitz
(Diagram 10—7)

Outside linebackers.   The outside linebackers are outside rushers responsible for blitz-and-peel pass coverage. Against two-back offensive sets, the strongside or tight-end-side linebacker has blitz-and-peel coverage on the first back that releases to the strong side. The weakside or open-side linebacker has blitz-and-peel coverage on the second back that releases to the weak side. If the offensive team lines up or motions to a one-back formation, both outside linebackers are responsible for blitz-and-peel coverage on the remaining back. If the back releases to the side of an outside linebacker, he covers him, and the linebacker away from the side of the release is a blitzing free rusher.

DIAGRAM 10–7
Eagle Strong Blitz

Two-Back Formation

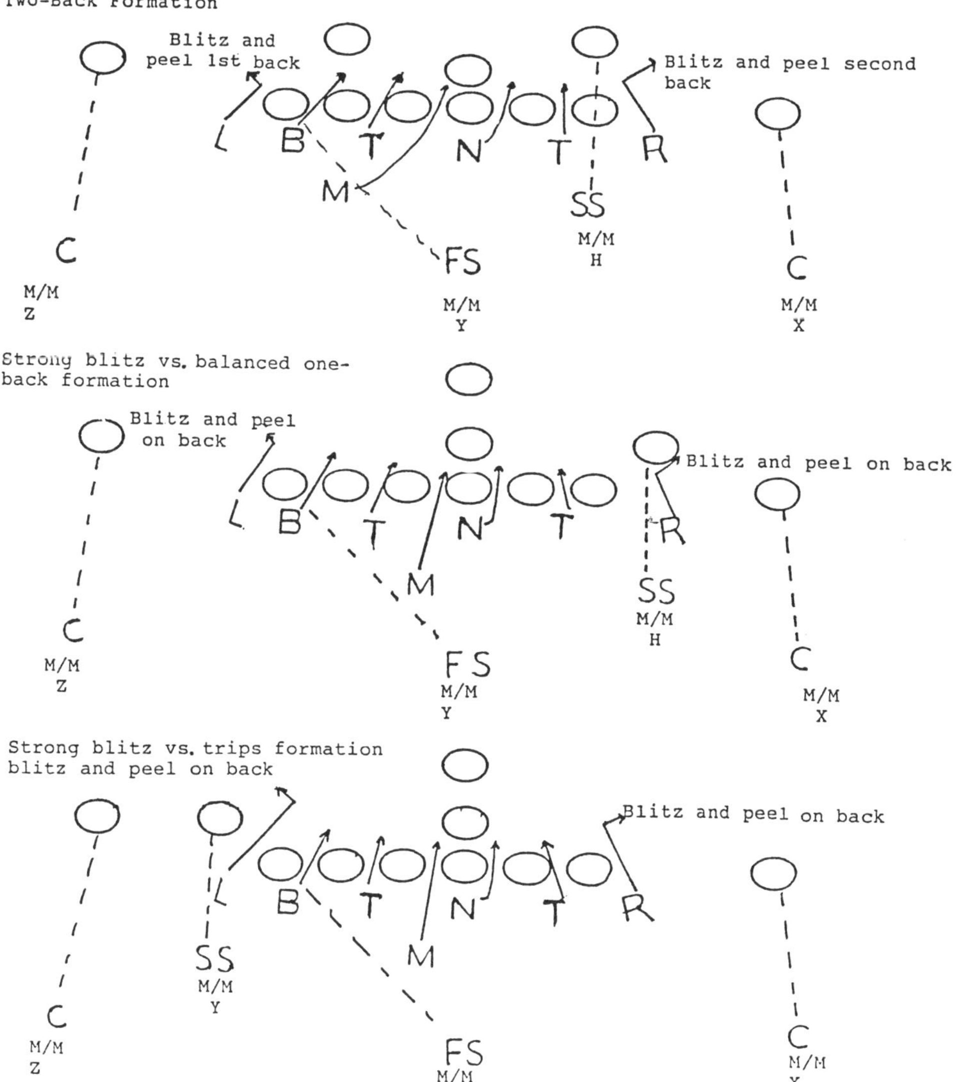

Note: Blitz and peel means the L and R blitz if their coverage does
not release on a pass route. If he releases on a route, they come off
their blitz and cover the back. On one-back formations L & R cover
the back if he releases to their side.

"B" linebacker.   The "B" linebacker blitzes through the "C" gap to the strong side of the formation.

Strong and weak tackles.   The tackles execute their normal Eagle charge low and hard through the "B" gap on their side of the formation.

Nose.   The Mac gives the nose a right or left call, sending him to the weakside "A" gap, or the "A" gap away from the tight end.

Mac linebacker.   The Mac linebacker blitzes the "A" gap to the tight end or strong side of the formation.

Strong safety.   The strong safety is responsible for man-for-man coverage on the H or the number-two receiver to the weak side against all formations except trips. Versus a trips formation, he has man-for-man coverage on the number-two receiver to the strong side of the formation.

Corners.   The corners have man-for-man coverage responsibility on the wide receivers, the X and the Z.

Free safety.   The free safety has man-for-man coverage responsibility on the number-two receiver to the strong side, usually the tight end, in all formations except trips. Versus a trips formation, the free safety has the number-three receiver to the strong side of the formation. This, again, is usually the tight end.

Eagle Middle Blitz
(Diagram 10—8)

Outside linebackers.   Same as strong blitz.

"B" linebacker.   The "B" linebacker has man-for-man coverage on the tight end with no possibility of help from any other defensive player.

Strong and weak tackles.   The strong and weak tackles penetrate hard in the "B" gap. They must work straight upfield and avoid getting collapsed by solid down blocks by the offensive tackles.

Nose.   The nose two-gaps the center. It is important that he get his hands on him, stay square, and not work to either side. He must allow the Mac and safety to clear as they blitz through the "A" gaps. After the Mac and strong safety clear, the nose becomes a lateral player, moving to always keep the ball in front of him.

Mac linebacker.   The Mac linebacker blitzes through the "A" gap to the strong side of the formation.

Strong safety.   Against two-back offensive formations, the strong safety blitzes through the weakside "A" gap. Versus a one-back balanced formation, the strong safety has man-for-man coverage on the number-two

DIAGRAM 10–8
Eagle Middle Blitz

Two-Back Formation
Nose two-gaps the Center,
stays square and keeps the
ball in front of him.

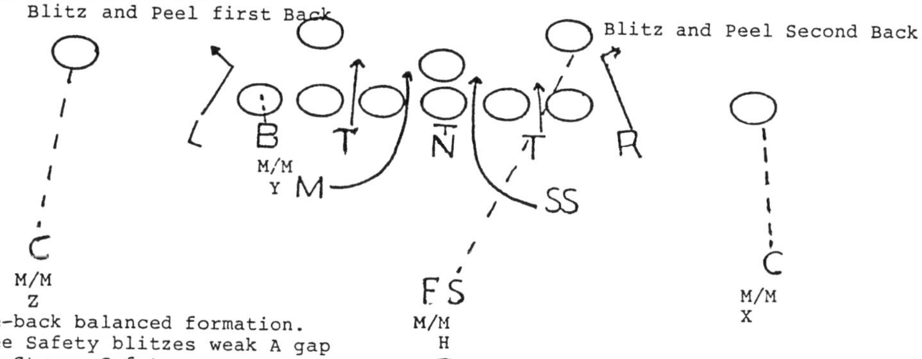

One-back balanced formation.
Free Safety blitzes weak A gap
and Strong Safety covers H man/man.

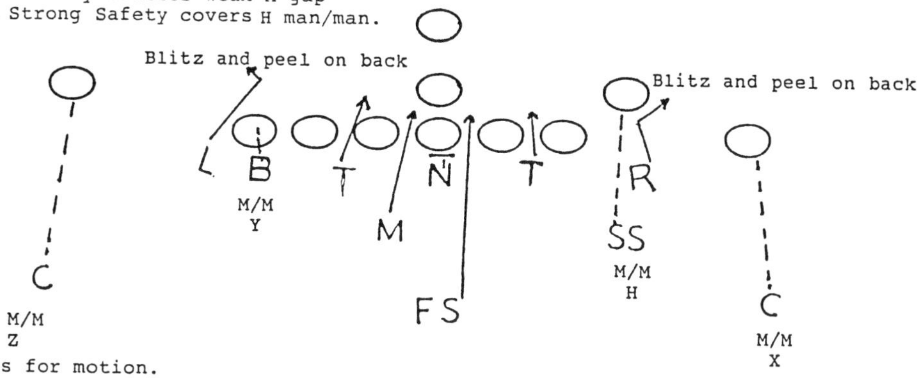

Trips for motion.
Free Safety blitzes weak A gap
and Strong Safety covers Y man/man.

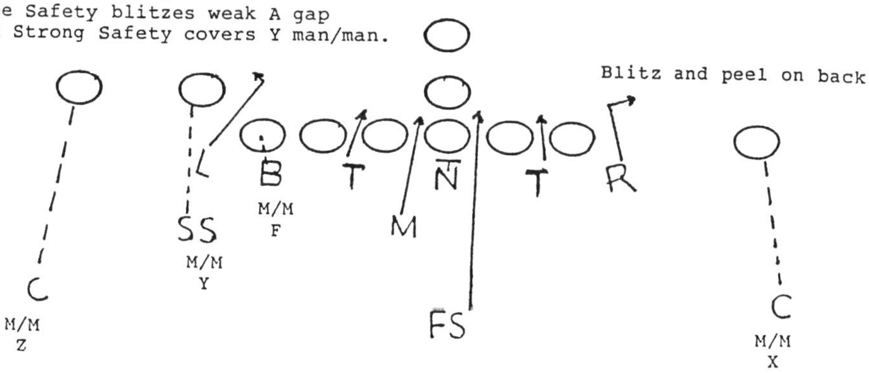

receiver to the weak side. Against trips formation, he is responsible for the number-two receiver to the strong side, man-for-man.

Corners.   The corners have man-for-man coverage responsibility on the wide receivers, the X and the Z.

Free safety.   The free safety is responsible for man-for-man coverage on the H or the number-two receiver weakside with two-back offensive formations. Against one-back sets, the free safety blitzes the weakside "A" gap just as he does when he is executing his one-back responsibilities when a safety dog is called.

The Eagle defense, by its alignment, has unlimited possibilities for dogs and blitzes. This defensive scheme allows for many effective ways to pressure the running and passing attacks of offensive teams. However, I feel they must be used discreetly, disguised, and mixed effectively with zone and man pass coverage.